SOPHOKLES

Sophokles (c. 496–405 BC) was an ancient Greek tragedian. Of his more than 120 plays, only seven have survived in a complete form: *Ajax, Antigone, Women of Trachis, Oedipus Rex, Electra, Philoctetes* and *Oedipus at Colonus*.

ANNE CARSON

Anne Carson was born in Canada and now lives partly in Iceland.

Sophokles

ELEKTRA

Translated by Anne Carson

NICK HERN BOOKS
London
www.nickhernbooks.co.uk

A Nick Hern Book

This English translation of *Elektra* first published in Great Britain in 2001 by Oxford University Press

Published in this edition in 2025 as a paperback original by Nick Hern Books Limited, The Glasshouse, 49a Goldhawk Road, London W12 8QP, by arrangement with Oxford University Press, for sale in the United Kingdom and the Commonwealth (excluding Canada), and not for export therefrom

This translation of *Elektra* copyright © 2001 Anne Carson
Textual notes copyright © 2001 Michael Shaw

Anne Carson has asserted her moral right to be identified as the translator of this work

Cover image of Brie Larson; photography by Helen Murray; artwork by Studio Doug

Designed and typeset by Nick Hern Books, London
Printed in the UK by CPI Group (UK) Ltd

A CIP catalogue record for this book is available from the British Library

ISBN 978 1 83904 446 5

CAUTION   All rights whatsoever in this play are strictly reserved. Requests to reproduce the text in whole or in part should be addressed to the publisher.

Applications for performance in any medium and in any language throughout the world should be addressed to Paradigm Talent Agency LLC (attn: Jamie Kaye-Phillips), *email* jkayephillips@paradigmagency.com, *tel* +1 917 671 1001

No performance of any kind may be given unless a licence has been obtained. Applications should be made before rehearsals begin. Publication of this play does not necessarily indicate its availability for performance.

This edition of *Elektra* in the English translation by Anne Carson was published alongside a new production by Empire Street Productions. It opened at the Theatre Royal Brighton on 13 January 2025, before transferring to the Duke of York's Theatre, London, on 5 February (previews from 24 January). The cast was as follows:

ELEKTRA	Brie Larson
CLYTEMNESTRA	Stockard Channing
CHRYSOTHEMIS	Marième Diouf
AEGISTHUS	Greg Hicks
ORESTES	Patrick Vaill
CHORUS	Hannah Bristow
CHORUS / UNDERSTUDY ELEKTRA	Wallis Currie-Wood
CHORUS	Jo Goldsmith-Eteson
CHORUS	Nardia Ruth
CHORUS / UNDERSTUDY CLYTEMNESTRA	Rebecca Thorn
CHORUS / UNDERSTUDY CHYSOTHEMIS	Adeola Yemitan
UNDERSTUDY ORESTES & AEGISTHUS	Arthur Boan

Director	Daniel Fish
Choreographer	Annie-B Parson
Set Designer	Jeremy Herbert
Costume Designer	Doey Lüthi
Lighting Designer	Adam Silverman
Sound Designer	Max & Ben Ringham
Composer	Ted Hearne

Characters

PAEDAGOGUS *or* OLD MAN, *servant and former tutor of Orestes*
ORESTES, *son of Clytemnestra and Agamemnon, King of Argos*
CHRYSOTHEMIS, *daughter of Clytemnestra and Agamemnon*
ELEKTRA, *daughter of Clytemnestra and Agamemnon*
CLYTEMNESTRA, *Queen of Argos*
AEGISTHUS, *paramour of Clytemnestra*
CHORUS *of Mycenaen women*
PYLADES, *Orestes' silent friend*

Line numbers in the right-hand margin of the text refer to the English translation only, and the notes on the text at p. 87 are keyed to these lines.

Scene: at Mycenae before the palace of Agamemnon.

Enter the OLD MAN *and* ORESTES *with* PYLADES.

PAEDAGOGUS.
You are his son! Your father
marshalled the armies at Troy once –
child of Agamemnon: look around you now.
Here is the land you were longing to see all that time.
Ancient Argos. You dreamed of this place.
The grove of Io, where the gadfly drove her.
Look, Orestes. There is the marketplace
named for Apollo,
wolfkiller god.
And on the left, the famous temple of Hera. 10
But stop! There – do you know what that is?
Mycenae. Yes. Look at it. Walls of gold!
Walls of death. It is the house of Pelops.
I got you out of there
out of the midst of your father's murder,
one day long ago.
From the hands of your sister
I carried you off. Saved your life. Reared you up –
to this: to manhood. To avenge your father's death.
So, Orestes! And you, dear 20
Pylades –
Now is the time to decide what to do.
Already the sun is hot upon us.
Birds are shaking, the world is awake.
Black stars and night have died away.
So before anyone is up and about
let's talk.
Now is no time to delay.
This is the edge of action.

ORESTES.

I love you, old man.
The signs of goodness shine from your face.
Like a thoroughbred horse – he gets old,
but he does not lose heart,
he pricks up his ears – so you
urge me forward
and stand on the front rank yourself.
Good. Now,
I will outline my plan. You
listen sharp.
If I'm off target anywhere,
set me straight.
You see, I went to Pytho
to ask the oracle how I could get justice
from the killers of my father.
Apollo answered:

Take no weapons.
No shield.
No army.
Go alone – a hand in the night.
Snare them.
Slaughter them.
You have the right.

That is the oracle.
Here is the plan:
you go into the house at the first chance.
Find out all that is happening there.
Find out and report to us. Be very clear.
You're so old, they won't know you.
And your garlands will fool them.
Now this is your story:
you're a stranger from Phocis,
from the house of Phanoteus
(he's the most powerful ally they have).
Tell them on oath that Orestes is dead.
An accident. Fatal:
rolled out of his chariot on the racetrack at Delphi.

Dragged to death under the wheels.
Let that be the story.
Meanwhile, we go to my father's grave,
as Apollo commanded,
to pour libation and crown tomb
with locks of hair cut from my head.
Then we'll be back
with that bronzeplated urn
(you know, the one I hid in the bushes).
Oh yes, we'll fool them
with this tale of me dead,
burnt,
nothing left but ash.
What good news for them!

As for me –
what harm can it do
to die in words?
I save my life and win glory besides!
Can a mere story be evil? No, of course not –
so long as it pays in the end.
I know of shrewd men
who die a false death
so as to come home
all the more valued.
Yes, I am sure:
I will stand clear of this lie
and break on my enemies like a star.

O land of my fathers! O gods of this place!
Take me in. Give me luck on this road.
House of my father:
I come to cleanse you with justice.
I come sent by gods.
Do not exile me from honour!
Put me in full command
of the wealth and the house!
Enough talk.
Old man, look to your task.
We are off.

This is the point on which everything hinges.
This is the moment of proof.

ELEKTRA (*a cry from inside the house*).
IO MOI MOI DYSTENOS.

OLD MAN.
What was that? I heard
a cry – some servant in the house?

ORESTES.
Can it be poor Elektra?
Should we stay here and listen?

OLD MAN.
No. Nothing precedes the work of Apollo.
That is our first step: your father's libations.
That is the way to win: action.

> *Exit* OLD MAN *and* ORESTES *with* PYLADES.
> *Enter* ELEKTRA *from the palace.*

ELEKTRA.
O holy light!
And equal air shaped on the world –
you hear my songs,
you hear the blows fall.
You know the blood runs
when night sinks away.   120
All night I watch.
All night I mourn,
in this bed that I hate in this house I detest.
How many times can a heart break?
Oh Father,
it was not killer Ares
who opened his arms
in some foreign land
to welcome you.
But my own mother and her lover Aegisthus: 130
those two good woodsmen
took an axe and split you down like an oak.
No pity for these things,

there is no pity
but mine,
oh Father,
for the pity of your butchering rawblood death.

Never
will leave off lamenting,
never. No.
As long as the stars sweep through heaven.
As long as I look on this daylight.
No.
Like the nightingale who lost her child
I will stand in his doorway
and call on his name.
Make then all hear.
Make this house echo.
O Hades!
Persephone!
Hermes of hell!
Furies, I call you!
Who watch
when lives are murdered.
Who watch when loves betray.
Come! Help me! Strike back!
Strike back for my father murdered!
And send my brother to me.
Because
alone,
the whole poised force of my life is nothing
against this.

Enter CHORUS.

CHORUS.
>Your mother is evil *strophe 1*
>but on my child why
>melt your life away in mourning?
>Why let grief eat you alive?
>It was long ago
>she took your father:

her hand came out of unholy dark
and cut him down. 170
I curse the one
who did the deed
(if this is right to say).

ELEKTRA.
You are women of noble instinct
and you come to console me
in my pain
I know.
I do understand.
But I will not let go this man or this mourning.

He is my father. 180
I cannot not grieve.
Oh my friends,
friendship is a tension. It makes delicate demands.
I ask this one thing:
let me go mad in my own way.

CHORUS. *antistrophe 1*
Not from Hades' black and universal lake can you lift him.
Not by groaning, not by prayers.
Yet you run yourself out
in grief with no cure,
no time limit, no measure. 190
It is a knot no one can untie.
Why are you so in love with
things unbearable?

ELEKTRA.
None but fool or an infant
could forget a father
gone so far and cold.
No.
Lament is a pattern cut and fitted around my mind —
like the bird who calls Itys! Itys! endlessly,
bird of grief, 200
angel of Zeus.
O heartdragging Niobe,

> I count you a god:
> buried in rock yet
> always you weep.

CHORUS.
> You are not the only one in the world *strophe 2*
> my child, who has stood in the glare of grief.
> Compare yourself:
> you go too far.
> Look at your sister, Chrysothemis:
> she goes on living. So does Iphianassa.
> And the boy – his secret years are sorrowful too,
> but he will be brilliant
> one day when Mycenae welcomes him home
> to his father's place, to his own land
> in the guidance of Zeus –
> Orestes!

ELEKTRA.
> Him yes!
> I am past exhaustion
> in waiting for him –
> no children,
> no marriage,
> no light in my heart.
> I live in a place of tears.
> And he
> simply forgets.
> Forgets what he suffered,
> forgets what he knew.
> Messages reach me, each one belied.
> He is passionate – as any lover.
> But his passion does not bring him here.

CHORUS.
> Have courage, *antistrophe 2*
> my child.
> Zeus is still great in heaven,
> he watches and governs all things.
> Leave this anger to Zeus: it burns too high in you.

Don't hate so much.
Nor let memory go.
For time is a god who can simplify all.
And as for Orestes 240
on the shore of Crisa
where oxen graze –
he does not forget you.
Nor is the king of death
on the banks of Acheron
unaware.

ELEKTRA.
But meanwhile most of my life has slid by
without hope.
I sink.
I melt. 250
Father has gone and there is no man left
who cares enough to stand up for me.
Like some beggar
wandered in off the street,
I serve as a slave
in the halls of my father.
Dressed in these rags,
I stand at the table
and feast on air.

CHORUS.
One rawblood cry *strophe 3* 260
on the day he returned,
one rawblood cry went through the halls
just as the axeblade
rose
and fell.
He was caught by guile,
cut down by lust:
together they bred a thing shaped like a monster –
god or mortal
no one knows. 270

ELEKTRA.
   That day tore out the nerves of my life.
   That night:
   far too silent the feasting,
   much too sudden
   the silence.
   My father looked up and saw
   death coming out of their hands.
   Those hands took my life hostage.
   Those hands murdered me.
   I pray 280
   the great god of Olympus
   give them pain on pain to pay for this!
   And smother the glow
   of deeds like these.

CHORUS.
   Think again, Elektra. *antistrophe 3*
   Don't say any more.
   Don't you see what you're doing?
   You make your own pain.
   Why keep wounding yourself?
   With so much evil stored up 290
   in that cold dark soul of yours

   you breed enemies everywhere you touch.
   But you must not
   clash with the people in power.

ELEKTRA.
   By dread things I am compelled. I know that.
   I see the trap closing.
   I know what I am.
   But while life is in me
   I will not stop this violence. No.
   Oh my friends 300
   who is there to comfort me?
   Who understands?
   Leave me be,
   let me go,

do not soothe me.
This is a knot no one can untie.
There will be no rest,
there is no retrieval.
No number exists for
griefs like these. 310

CHORUS.
Yes but I speak from concern – *epode*
as a mother would: trust me.
Do not breed violence out of violence.

ELEKTRA.
Alright then, you tell me one thing –
at what point does the evil level off in my life?
You say ignore the deed – is that right?
Who could approve this?
It defies human instinct!
Such ethics make no sense to me.
And how could I nestle myself in a life of ease 320

while my father lies out in the cold,
outside honour?
My cries are wings:
they pierce the cage.
For if a dead man is earth and nothing,
if a dead man is void and dead space lying,
if a dead man's murderers
do not give
blood for blood
to pay for this, 330
then shame does not exist.
Human reverence
is gone.

CHORUS.
I came here, child, because I care
for your welfare as my own.
But perhaps I am wrong.
Let it be as you say.

ELEKTRA.
Women, I am ashamed before you: I know
you find me extreme
in my grief. 340
I bear it hard.
But I tell you I have no choice.
It compels. I act because it compels.
Oh forgive me. But how could I –
how could a woman of any nobility
stand
and watch her father's house go bad?
There is something bad here,
growing. Day and night
I watch it. Growing. 350

My mother is where it begins.
She and I are at war.
Our relation is hatred.
And I live in this house
with my father's own killers:
they rule me. They dole out my life.
What kind of days do you think I have here?
I see my father's throne
with Aegisthus on it.
I see my father's robes 360
with Aegisthus in them.
I see my father's hearth with Aegisthus presiding –
right where he stood when he struck
my father down!
And the final outrage:
the killer tucked in my father's bed.
Behold the man who pleasures my mother –
should I call that thing 'Mother' that lies at his side?
God! Her nerve astounds me.
She lives with that polluted object, 370
fearing no fury. No,
she laughs!
Celebrates
that day – the day she took my father

with dances and song and slaughter of sheep!
A monthly bloodgift to the gods who keep her safe.

I watch
all going dark in the rooms of my house.
I weep.
I melt.

I grieve
for the strange cruel feast made in my father's name.
But I grieve to myself:
not allowed even to shed the tears I would.
No – that creature
who calls herself noble
will shriek at me:
'Godcursed! You piece of hatred!
So you've lost your father – is that unique?
No mortal mourns but you?
Damn you.
May the gods of hell damn you
to groan perpetually there
as you groan
perpetually
here!'
That's her style –
and when she hears someone mention Orestes,
then she goes wild, comes screaming at me:
'Have I you to thank for this?

Isn't it your work? Wasn't it you
who stole Orestes out of my hands
and smuggled him away?
You'll pay for it.
I tell you, you will pay.'
Howling bitch. And by her side
the brave bridegroom –
this lump of bad meat.
With women only
he makes his war.

And I wait.
I wait.
I wait.
for Orestes.
He will come! He will end this.
But my life is dying out.
He is always on the verge of doing something
then does nothing.
He has worn out all the hopes I had or could have.
Oh my friends, 420
in times like these,
self-control has no meaning.
Rules of reverence do not apply.
Evil is a pressure that shapes us to itself.

CHORUS.
Is Aegisthus at home?

ELEKTRA.
No. Do you think I'd be
standing outdoors?
He is gone to the fields.

CHORUS.
That gives me courage
to say what I came to say. 430

ELEKTRA.
What is it you want?

CHORUS.
I want to know – your brother –
do you say he is coming? Or has a plan?

ELEKTRA.
Yes, he says so. But he says a lot. Does nothing.

CHORUS.
A man who does a great deed may hesitate.

ELEKTRA.
Oh? I saved his life without hesitating.

CHORUS.
Courage. His nature is good, he will not fail his kin.

ELEKTRA.
That belief is what keeps me alive.

CHORUS.
Quiet now. Here is your sister come from the house,
Chrysothemis, of the same father 440
and mother as you.
She has offerings in her hands,
as if for dead.

Enter CHRYSOTHEMIS *carrying garlands and a vessel.*

CHRYSOTHEMIS.
Here you are again at the doorway, sister,
telling your tale to the world!
When will you learn?
It's pointless. Pure self-indulgence.
Yes, I know how bad things are.
I suffer too – if I had the strength
I would show what I think of them. 450
But now is not the right time.
In rough waters, lower the sail, is my theory.
Why pretend to be doing,
unless I can do some real harm?
I wish you would see this.
And yet,
it is true,
justice is not on my side.
Your choice is the right one. On the other hand,
if I want to live a free woman, 460
there are masters who must be obeyed.

ELEKTRA.
You appall me.
Think of the father who sired you! But you do not.
All your thought is for her.
These sermons you give me are all learnt
from Mother, not a word is your own.

Well it's time for you to make a choice:
quit being 'sensible'
or keep your good sense and betray your own kin.
Wasn't it you who just said, 470
'If I had strength I would show how I hate them!'
Yet here I am doing everything possible
to avenge our father,
and do you help? No!
You try to turn me aside.
Isn't this simply cowardice added to evil?
Instruct me – no! Let me tell you:
what do I stand to gain if I cease my lament?
Do I not live? Badly, I know, but I live.
What is more, 480
I am a violation to them.
And so, honour the dead –
if any grace exists down there.
Now
you hate them, you say.
But this hate is all words.
In fact, you live with the killers.
And I tell you,
if someone were to give me
all the gifts that make your days delicious, 490
I would not bend. No.
You can have your rich table
and life flowing over the cup.
I need one food:
I must not violate Elektra.
As for your status, I couldn't care less.
Nor would you, if you had any self-respect.
You could have been called
child of the noblest men!
Instead they call you mother's girl, 500
they think you base.
Your own dead father,
your own loved ones,
you do betray.

CHORUS.
> No anger I pray.
> There is profit for both
> if you listen to one another.

CHRYSOTHEMIS.
> Her talk is no surprise to me, ladies.
> I'm used to this.
> And I wouldn't have bothered 510
> to speak at all, expect –
> for the rumour I heard.
> There is very great evil coming this way,
> something to cut her long laments
> short.

ELEKTRA.
> Tell me what is the terrible thing?
> If it is worse than my present life,
> I give up.

CHRYSOTHEMIS.
> I tell them what I know:
> they plan, 520
> unless you cease from this mourning,
> to send you where you will not see the sun again.
> You'll be singing your songs
> alive
> in a room
> in the ground.
> Think about that.
> And don't blame me when you suffer.
> Too late then.
> Now is the time to start being sensible. 530

ELEKTRA.
> Ah. That is their intention, is it.

CHRYSOTHEMIS.
> It is. As soon as Aegisthus comes home.

ELEKTRA.
> May he come soon, then.

CHRYSOTHEMIS.
   What are you saying?

ELEKTRA.
   Let him come, if he has his plan ready.

CHRYSOTHEMIS.
   What do you mean? Are you losing your mind?

ELEKTRA.
   I want to escape from you all.

CHRYSOTHEMIS.
   Not go on living?

ELEKTRA.
   Living? Oh yes
   my life is a beautiful thing, is it not.   540

CHRYSOTHEMIS.
   Well it could be, if you got some sense.

ELEKTRA.
   Don't bother telling me to betray those I love.

CHRYSOTHEMIS.
   I tell you we have masters, we must bend.

ELEKTRA.
   You bend – you go ahead and lick their boots.
   It's not my way.

CHRYSOTHEMIS.
   Don't ruin your life in sheer stupidity.

ELEKTRA.
   I will ruin my life, if need be,
   avenging our father.

CHRYSOTHEMIS.
   But our father, I know, forgives us for this.

ELEKTRA.
   Cowards' talk.   550

CHRYSOTHEMIS.
   You won't listen to reason at all, will you?

ELEKTRA.
   No. My mind is my own.

CHRYSOTHEMIS.
   Well then I'll be on my way.

ELEKTRA.
   Where are you going? Whose offerings are those?

CHRYSOTHEMIS.
   Mother is sending me to Father's tomb,
   to pour libation.

ELEKTRA.
   What? To her mortal enemy?

CHRYSOTHEMIS.
   To her 'murder victim', as you like to say.

ELEKTRA.
   Whose idea was this?

CHRYSOTHEMIS.
   It came out of a dream in the night, I believe. 560

ELEKTRA.
   Gods of my father be with me now!

CHRYSOTHEMIS.
   You take courage from a nightmare?

ELEKTRA.
   Tell the dream and I'll answer you.

CHRYSOTHEMIS.
   There is little to tell.

ELEKTRA.
   Tell it anyway.
   Little words can mean
   death or life sometimes.

CHRYSOTHEMIS.
Well the story is
she dreamed of our father
and knew him again 570
for he came back into the light.
Then she saw him take hold of his sceptre
and stick it in the hearth –
his own sceptre from the old days,
that Aegisthus carries now.
And from the sceptre sprang a branch
in full climbing leaf
which cast a shadow over the whole land of Mycenae.
That is as much as I got
from one who overheard her 580
telling the dream to the sun.
More I don't know, except
fear is her reason for sending me out today.
So I beg you, by the gods of our family,
listen to me.
Don't throw your life away on plain stupidity.
For if you spurn me now,
you'll come begging later
when the trouble starts.

ELEKTRA.
Oh dear one, no. 590
You cannot touch this tomb
with any of those things you have in your hands.
It breaks the law. It would be unholy
to bring that woman's libations
to our father: she is the enemy.
No. Pitch them to the winds
or down a dark hole.
They shall come nowhere near his resting place.
But when she dies and goes below,
she will find them waiting. 600
Treasure keeps, down there.

God! Her nerve is astounding.
What woman alive would send gifts

to garnish her own murder victim?
And do you imagine
the dead man would welcome such
honours
from the hand of the woman who butchered him –
think! To clean her blade she wiped it off on his head!
You astonish me – do you really believe 610
such gifts will cancel murder?
Throw them away.
Here, instead
cut a lock from your hair
and a lock of mine – meagre gifts
but it is all I have.
Take this to him, the hair
and this belt of mine,
though it's nothing elaborate.
Kneel down there and pray to him. 620
Pray he come up from the ground
to stand with us against our enemies.
Pray that his son Orestes live
to trample his enemies underfoot.
And someday you and I will go in better style than this
to crown his tomb.
But I wonder. You know
I wonder –
suppose he had some part
in sending her these cold unlucky dreams. 630

Well, never mind that.
Sister,
do this deed.
Stand up for yourself
and for me and for this man we love
more than anyone else in the world,
this dead man. Your father. My father.

CHORUS.
The girl speaks for human reverence.
And you,
if you have any sense, will do what she says. 640

ELEKTRA 27

CHRYSOTHEMIS.
> I will do it. It is the right thing,
> why dispute?
> But please, my friends,
> I need silence from you.
> If my mother finds out,
> the attempt will turn bitter for me,
> I fear.

Exit CHRYSOTHEMIS.

CHORUS.
> Unless I am utterly wrong in my reading of omens   *strophe*
> unless I am out of my mind
> Justice is coming   650
> with clear signs before her
> and righteousness in her hands.
> She is coming down on us, child, coming now!
> There is courage
> whispering into me
> when I hear tell of these sweetbreathing dreams.
> He does not forget –
> the one who begot you
> the king of the Greeks.
> She does not forget –   660
> the jaw that bit him in two:
> ancient and sharpened on both sides to butcher the meat!
>
> Vengeance is coming – her hands like an   *antistrophe*
>   army
> her feet as a host.
> She will come out of hiding
> come scorching down
> on love that is filth
> and beds that are blood
> where marriage should never have happened!
> Conviction   670
> is strong in me:
> visions like these are no innocent sign for killers.
> I say no omens exist

for mortals to read
from the cold faces of dreams
or from oracles
unless this fragment of death steps into the daylight.

O horserace of Pelops, *epode*
once long ago
you came in the shape of a wide calamity 680
to this land.
And from the time when
Myrtilus pitched and sank in the sea
his solid-gold life
sliced off at the roots –
never
since that time
has this house
got itself clear of
rawblood 690
butchery.

Enter CLYTEMNESTRA.

CLYTEMNESTRA.
Prowling the streets again, are you?
Of course, with Aegisthus away.
He was always the one
who kept you indoors where you couldn't embarrass us.
Now that he's gone you pay no heed to me.
Yet you love to make me the text of your lectures:
What an arrogant bitchminded tyrant I am,
a living insult to you and your whole way of being!
But do I in fact insult you? No. I merely return 700
the muck you throw at me.
Father, Father, Father! Your perpetual excuse –
your father got his death from me. From me! That's right!
I make no denial.
It was Justice who took him, not I alone.
And you should have helped if you had any conscience.
For this father of yours,
this one you bewail,

this unique Greek,
had the heart to sacrifice your own sister to the gods. 710

And how was that? Did he have some share
in the pain of her birth? No – I did it myself!
Tell me:
why did he cut her throat? What was the reason?
You say for the Argives?
But they had no business to kill what was mine.
To save Menelaus?
Then I deserved recompense, wouldn't you say?
Did not Menelaus have children himself –
in fact two of them, 720
who ought to have died before mine
in all fairness?
Their mother, let's not forget,
was the cause of the whole expedition!
Or was it that Hades conceived some peculiar desire
to feast on my children instead?
Or perhaps
that murdering thug your father,
simply overlooked my children
in his tender care for Menelaus'. 730
Was that not brutal? Was that not perverse?

I say it was.
No doubt you disagree.
But I tell you one thing, that murdered girl
would speak for me if she had a voice.
Anyway, the deed is done.
I feel no remorse.
You think me degenerate?
Here's my advice:
perfect yourself
before you blame others. 740

ELEKTRA.
At least you can't say I started it this time;
these ugly remarks are unprovoked.
But I want to get a few things clear

about the dead man and my sister as well.
If you allow me.

CLYTEMNESTRA.
Go ahead, by all means. Begin this way more often
and we won't need ugly remarks at all, will we?

ELEKTRA.
All right then. Yes.
You killed my father, you admit. 750
What admission could bring more shame?
Never mind if it was legal or not – did you care?
Let's talk facts: there was only one reason you killed him.
You were seduced by that creature you live with.
Ask Artemis,
goddess of hunters,
why she stopped the winds at Aulis.
No, I'll tell you:
my father one day, so I hear,
was out in the grove of the goddess. 760
The sound of his footfall startled a stag out from cover
and, when he killed it, he let fall a boast.
This angered the daughter of Leto.
She held the Achaeans in check until,
as payment for the animal,
my father should offer his own daughter.
Hence, the sacrifice. There was no other way.
He had to free the army,
to sail home or towards Troy.
These were the pressures that closed upon him. 770

He resisted, he hated it –
and then he killed her.
Not for Menelaus' sake, no, not at all.
But even if – let's say we grant your claim –
he did these things to help his brother,
was it right he should die for it at your hands?
By what law?
Watch out: this particular law
could recoil upon your own head.

If we made it a rule   780
to answer killing with killing,
you would die first,
in all justice.
Open your eyes! The claim is a fake.
Tell me:
why do you live this way?
Your life is filth.
You share your bed with a bloodstained man:
once he obliged you by killing my father,
now you put him to use making children.   790
Once you had *decent* children from a *decent* father,
now you've thrown them out.
Am I supposed to praise that?
Or will you say
you do all this to avenge your child?
The thought is obscene –
to bed your enemies
and use a daughter as an alibi!
Oh why you go on? I can't argue with you.
You have your one same answer ready: 800
'*That's no way to talk to your mother!*'

Strange.
I don't think of you as mother at all.
You are some sort of punishment cage
locked around my life.
Evils from you, evils from him
are the air I breathe.
And what of Orestes? – he barely escaped you.
Poor boy.
The minutes are grinding him away somewhere.   810
You always accuse me
of training him up to be an avenger –

Oh I would if I could, you're so right!
Proclaim it to all!

Call me
baseminded, blackmouthing bitch! if you like –

32 ELEKTRA

for if this is my nature
we know how I come by it, don't we?

CHORUS (*looking at* CLYTEMNESTRA).
Look. Anger is breathing out of her.
Yet she seems not to care 820
about right and wrong.

CLYTEMNESTRA.
Right and wrong!
What use is that in dealing with her?
Do you hear her insults?
And this girl is old enough to know better.
That fact is, she would do *anything*,
don't you see that?
No shame at all.

ELEKTRA.
Ah now there you mistake me.
Shame I do feel. 830
And I know there is something all wrong about me –
believe me. Sometimes I shock myself.
But there is a reason: you.
You never let up
this one same pressure of hatred on my life:
I am the shape you made me.
Filth teaches filth.

CLYTEMNESTRA.
You little animal.
I and my deeds and my words draw
far too much comment from you. 840

ELEKTRA.
You said it, not I.
For the deeds are your own.
But deeds find words for themselves,
don't they?

CLYTEMNESTRA.
By Artemis I swear, you will pay for this
when Aegisthus comes home!

ELEKTRA.
> See? You're out of control.
> Though you gave me permission to say what I want,
> you don't know how to listen.

CLYTEMNESTRA.
> Silence! If you allow me 850
> I will proceed with my sacrifice.
> You spoke your piece.

ELEKTRA.
> Please! By all means! Go to it.
> Not another word from me.

CLYTEMNESTRA (*to her* ATTENDANT).
> You there! Yes you – lift up
> these offerings for me.
> I will offer prayers to this our king
> and loosen the fears that hold me now.
> Do you hear me, Apollo?
> I call you my champion! 860
> But my words are guarded, for I am not among friends.
> It wouldn't do to unfold the whole tale
> with her standing here.
> She has a destroying tongue in her
> and she does love
> to sow wild stories all over town.
> So listen, I'll put it this way:
> last night was a night of bad dreams
> and ambiguous visions.
> If they bode well for me, Lycian king, bring them to pass. 870
> Otherwise, roll them back on my enemies!
> And if there are certain people around
> plotting to pull me down
> from the wealth I enjoy,
> do not allow it.
> I want everything to go on as it is,
> untroubled.
> It suits me – this grand palace life
> in the midst of my loved ones

and children – at least the ones 880
who do not bring me hatred and pain.

These are my prayers, Apollo.
Hear them.
Apollo,
grant them.
Gracious to all of us as we petition you.
And for the rest, though I keep silent,
I credit you with knowing it fully.
You are a god.
It goes without saying, 890
the children of Zeus see all things.
Amen.

Enter OLD MAN.

OLD MAN.
Ladies, can you tell me for certain
if this is the house of Aegisthus the King?

CHORUS.
Yes, stranger, it is.

OLD MAN.
And am I correct that this is his wife?
She has a certain royal look.

CHORUS.
Yes. That's who she is.

OLD MAN.
Greetings, Queen. I have come with glad tidings
For you and Aegisthus, from a friend of yours. 900

CLYTEMNESTRA.
That's welcome news. But tell me
who sent you.

OLD MAN.
Phanoteus the Phocian. On a mission of some
importance.

ELEKTRA 35

CLYTEMNESTRA.
> What mission? Tell me.
> Insofar as I like Phanoteus,
> I am likely to like your news.

OLD MAN.
> Orestes is dead. That is the sum of it.

ELEKTRA.
> OI 'GO TALAINA.
> My death begins now.

CLYTEMNESTRA.
> What are you saying, what are you saying? 910
> Don't bother with her.

OLD MAN.
> Orestes – dead. I say it again.

ELEKTRA.
> I am at the end. I exist no more.

CLYTEMNESTRA (*to* ELEKTRA).
> Mind your own affairs, girl.
> But you, stranger – tell me the true story:
> how did he die?

OLD MAN.
> Yes I was sent for this purpose, I'll tell the whole thing.
> Well:
> he had gone to the spectacle at Delphi,
> where all Greece turns up for the games. 920
> Things were just beginning to get under way
> and the herald's voice rang out
> announcing the footrace – first contest.
> When he came onto the track
> he was radiant. Every eye turned.
> Well, he levelled the competition,
> took first prize and came away famous.
> Oh there's so much to tell –
> I never saw anything like his performance! – but
> let me come straight to the point. 930

He won every contest the judges announced –
single lap, double lap, pentathlon, you name it.

First prize every time.
He was beginning to take on an aura.
His name rang out over the track again and again:
'Argive Orestes,
whose father commanded the armies of Greece!'
So far so good.
But when a god sends harm,
no man can sidestep it, 940
no matter how strong he may be.
Came another day.
Sunrise: the chariot race.
He entered the lists.
What a pack:
there was one from Achaea,
a Spartan,
two Libyan drivers,
and he in the midst on Thessalian horses
stood fifth. 950
Sixth an Aetolian man, driving bays.
Seventh someone from Magnesia.
An Aenian man, riding white horses, had eighth place
and ninth a driver from godbuilt Athens.
Then a Boeotian.
Ten cars in all.
As they took their positions,
the judges cast lots to line up the cars.
A trumpet blast sounded.
They shot down the track. 960
All shouting together, reins tossing –

a hard clatter filled the whole course
and a vast float of dust,
as they all streamed together,
each one lashing and straining ahead
to the next axle box, the next snorting lip,
and the horse-foam flying
back over shoulders and wheels as they pounded past.

ELEKTRA 37

Meanwhile Orestes
just grazing the post each time with his wheel, 970
was letting his right horse go wide,
reining back on the other.
The cars were all upright at this point —

then all of a sudden
the Aenian's colts go out of control
and swerve off
just as they round the seventh turn.
They crash head-on into the Barcaean team.
Then one car after another comes ramming into the pile
and the whole plain of Crisa 980
fills with the smoke of wrecks.
Now
the Athenian driver was smart, he saw

what was happening.
Drew offside and waited as
the tide of cars went thundering by.
Orestes
was driving in last place,
lying back on his mares.
He had put his faith on the finish. 990
But as soon as he sees
the Athenian driver alone on the track

he lets out a cry that shivers his horses' ears
and goes after him.
Neck and neck
they are racing,
first one, then
the other
nosing ahead,
easing ahead. 1000

Now our unlucky boy had stood every course so far,
sailing right on in his upright car,
but at this point he lets the left rein go slack
with the horses turning,
he doesn't notice,

    hits the pillar and
    smashes the axle box in two.

    Out he flips
    over the chariot rail,
    reins snarled around him   1010
    and as he falls
    the horses scatter midcourse.
    They see him down. A gasp goes through the crowd:
    'Not the boy!'
    To go for glory and end like this –
    pounded against the ground,
    legs beating the sky –
    the other drivers could hardly manage
    to stop his team and cut him loose.
    Blood everywhere.   1020
    He was unrecognisable. Sickening.
    They burned him at once on a pyre
    and certain Phocians are bringing
    the might body back –
    just ashes,
    a little bronze urn –
    so you can bury him in his father's ground.
    That is my story.
    So far as words go,
    gruesome enough.   1030
    But for those who watched it,
    and we did watch it,
    the ugliest evil I ever saw.

CHORUS.
    PHEU PHEU.
    The whole ancient race
    torn off at the roots. Gone.

CLYTEMNESTRA.
    Zeus! What now? Should I call this good news?
    Or a nightmare cut to my own advantage?
    There is something grotesque
    in having my own evils save my life.   1040

ELEKTRA 39

OLD MAN.
What are you so disheartened at this news, my lady?

CLYTEMNESTRA.
To give birth is terrible, incomprehensible.
No matter how you suffer,
you cannot hate a child you've born.

OLD MAN.
My coming was futile then, it seems.

CLYTEMNESTRA.
Futile? Oh no. How –
if you've come with convincing proof of his death?
He was alive because I gave him life.
But he chose to desert my breasts and my care,
to live as an exile, aloof and strange. 1050
After he left here he never saw me.
But he laid against me
the death of his father,
he made terrible threats.
And I had no shelter in sleep by night or sleep by day:
Time stood like a deathmaster over me,
letting the minutes drop.
Now I am free!
Today I shake loose from my fear
of her, my fear of him. 1060
And to tell you the truth,
she did more damage.
She lived in my house
and drank
my lifeblood neat!
Now things are different.
She may go on making threats – but so what?
From now on, I pass my days in peace.

ELEKTRA.
OIMOI TALAINA.
Now I have grief enough to cry out OIMOI – 1070
Orestes! Poor cold thing.
As you lie in death

your own mother insults you.
What a fine sight!

CLYTEMNESTRA.
Well you're no fine sight.
But he looks as fine as can be.

ELEKTRA.
Nemesis! Hear her!

CLYTEMNESTRA.
Nemesis *has* heard me. And she has answered.

ELEKTRA.
Batter away. This is your hour of luck.

CLYTEMNESTRA.
And you think you will stop me, you and Orestes?

ELEKTRA.
It is we who are stopped. There's no stopping you.

CLYTEMNESTRA.
Stranger, you deserve reward
if you really have put a stop on her travelling tongue.

OLD MAN.
Then I'll be on my way, if all is well.

CLYTEMNESTRA.
Certainly not! You've earned better
of me and the man who dispatched you.
No, you go inside.
Just leave her out here
to go on with her evil litany.

Exit CLYTEMNESTRA *and* OLD MAN *into house.*

ELEKTRA.
Well how did she look to you – shattered by grief?
Heartbroken mother bewailing her only son?
No – you saw her – she went off laughing!
O TALAIN'EGO.
Orestes beloved,

ELEKTRA 41

as you die you destroy me.
You have torn away the part of my mind
where hope was –
my one hope in you
to live,
to come back, 1100
to avenge us.
Now where can I go?
Alone I am.
Bereft of you. Bereft of Father.
Should I go back into slavery?
Back to those creatures who cut down my father?
What a fine picture.
No.
I will not go back inside that house.
No. At this door 1110
I will let myself lie
unloved.
I will wither my life.
If it aggravates them,
they can kill me.
Yes it will be a grace if I die.
To exist is pain.
Life is no desire of mine any more.

CHORUS.
  Where are you lightnings of Zeus! *strophe 1*
  Where are you scorching Sun! 1120
  In these dark pits you leave us dark!

ELEKTRA.
  E E AIAI.

CHORUS.
  Child, why do you cry?

ELEKTRA.
  PHEU.

CHORUS.
  Don't make that sound.

ELEKTRA.
> You will break me.

CHORUS.
> How?

ELEKTRA.
> If you bring me hope and I know he is dead,
> you will harm my heart.

CHORUS.
> But think of Amphiaraus: *antistrophe 1* 1130
> he was a king once,
> snared by a woman in nets of gold.
> Now under the earth

ELEKTRA.
> E E IO.

CHORUS.
> He is a king in the shadows of souls.

ELEKTRA.
> PHEU.

CHORUS.
> Cry PHEU, yes! For his murderess –

ELEKTRA.
> was destroyed!

CHORUS.
> Destroyed.

ELEKTRA.
> I know – because an avenger arose. 1140
> I have no such person. That person is gone.

CHORUS.
> You are a woman marked for sorrow. *strophe 2*

ELEKTRA.
> Yes I know sorrow. Know it far too well.
> My life is a tunnel

ELEKTRA 43

choked
by the sweepings of dread.

CHORUS.
We have watched you grieving.

ELEKTRA.
Then do not try –

CHORUS.
What?

ELEKTRA.
To console me. 1150
The fact is,
there are no more hopes.
No fine brothers.
No comfort.

CHORUS.
Death exists inside every mortal. *antistrophe 2*

ELEKTRA.
Oh yes, but think of the hooves drumming down on him!
See that thing
dragging behind in the reins –

CHORUS.
Too cruel.

ELEKTRA.
Yes, Death made him a stranger – 1160

CHORUS.
PAPAI.

ELEKTRA.
Laid out
somewhere
not by my hands.
Not with my tears.

Enter CHRYSOTHEMIS.

CHRYSOTHEMIS.
  I am so happy, I ran here to tell you –
  putting good manners aside!
  I have good news for you that spells release
  from all your grieving.

ELEKTRA.
  Where could you find anything to touch my grief?   1170
  It has no cure.

CHRYSOTHEMIS.
  Orestes is with us – yes! Know if from me –

  plain as you see me standing here!

ELEKTRA.
  You are mad.
  You are joking.

CHRYSOTHEMIS.
  By the hearth of our father, this is no joke.
  He is with us. He is.

ELEKTRA.
  You poor girl.
  Who gave you this story?

CHRYSOTHEMIS.
  No one gave me the story!   1180
  I saw the evidence with my own eyes.

ELEKTRA.
  What evidence?
  My poor girl, what has set you on fire?

CHRYSOTHEMIS.
  Well listen, for gods' sake.
  Find out if I'm crazy or not.

ELEKTRA.
  All right, tell the tale, if it makes you happy.

CHRYSOTHEMIS.
  Yes, I will tell all I saw.

ELEKTRA 45

Well
When I arrived at Father's grave
I saw milk dripping down from the top of the mound 1190
and the tomb wreathed in flowers –
flowers of every kind – what a shock!
I peered all around –
in case someone was sneaking up on me
but no, the whole place was perfectly still.
I crept near the tomb.
And there it was.
Right there on the edge.
A lock of hair, fresh cut.
As soon as I saw it, a bolt went through me – 1200
almost as if I saw his face,
I suddenly knew! Orestes.
Beloved Orestes.
I lifted it up. I said not a word.
I was weeping for joy.
And I know it now as I knew it then,
this offering had to come from him.
Who else would bother, except you or me?
And I didn't do it. I'm sure of that.
You couldn't do it – god knows you don't 1210
take a step from this house without getting in trouble.
And certainly Mother has no such inclinations.

If she did, we would hear of it.
No, I tell you these offerings came from Orestes.
Oh Elektra, lift your heart!
Bad luck can't last forever.
Long have we lived in shadows and shuddering:
today I think our future is opening out.

ELEKTRA.
PHEU!
Poor lunatic. I feel sorry for you. 1220

CHRYSOTHEMIS.
What do you mean? Why aren't you happy?

ELEKTRA.
You're dreaming, girl, lost in moving dream.

CHRYSOTHEMIS.
Dreaming! How? I saw what I saw!

ELEKTRA.
He is dead, my dear one.
He's not going to save you.
Dead, do you hear me? Dead. Forget him.

CHRYSOTHEMIS.
OIMOI TALAINA.
Who told you that?

ELEKTRA.
Someone who was there when he died.

CHRYSOTHEMIS.
And where is this someone? It's all so strange.

ELEKTRA.
He's gone in the house. To entertain Mother.

CHRYSOTHEMIS.
I don't want to hear this. I don't understand.
Who put those offerings on father's tomb?

ELEKTRA.
I think, most likely, someone who wished
to honour Orestes' memory.

CHRYSOTHEMIS.
What a fool I am – here I come racing for joy
to tell you my news, with no idea
how things really are.
The evils multiply.

ELEKTRA.
Yes they do. But listen to me.
You could ease our sorrow.

CHRYSOTHEMIS.
How? Raise the dead?

ELEKTRA.
That's not what I meant. I am not quite insane.

CHRYSOTHEMIS.
Then what do you want? Am I capable of it?

ELEKTRA.
All you need is the nerve – to do what I say.

CHRYSOTHEMIS.
If it benefits us, I will not refuse.

ELEKTRA.
But you know nothing succeeds without work.

CHRYSOTHEMIS.
I do. I'll give you all the strength I have.

ELEKTRA.
Good then, listen. Here is my plan.
You know, I think, our present contingent of allies: 1250
zero. Death took them.
We two are alone.
Up to now, while I heard that my brother was living
I cherished a hope
that he'd arrive one day to avenge his father.
But Orestes
no longer exists. I look to you.
You will not shrink back.
You will stand with your sister
and put to death the man who murdered your father: 1260
Aegisthus.
After all, what are you waiting for?
Let's be blunt, girl, what hope is left?
Your losses are mounting,
the property gone and
marriage
seems a fading dream at your age –
or do you still console yourself with thoughts of a husband?
Forget it. Aegisthus is not so naive 1270
as to see children born from you or from me –

unambiguous grief for himself.
But now if you join in my plans,
you will win, in the first place,
profound and sacred respect from the dead below:
your father, your brother.
And second, people will call you noble.
That is your lineage, that is your future.
And besides, you will find a husband,
a good one: men like a woman with character. 1280
Oh don't you see? You'll make us famous!
People will cheer! They'll say
'Look at those two!' they'll say
'Look at the way they saved their father's house!
Against an enemy standing strong!
Risked their lives! Stood up to murder!
Those two deserve to be honoured in public,
on every streetcorner and festival in the city –
there should be a prize for heroism like that!'
So they will speak of us. 1290
And whether we live or die doesn't matter:
that fame will stand.
Oh my dear one, listen to me.
Take on your father's work,
take up your brother's task,
make some refuge from evil for me
and for you.
Because you know,
there is a kind of excellence
in me and you – born in us – 1300
and it cannot live in shame.

CHORUS.

In times like these, speaking or listening,
forethought is your ally.

CHRYSOTHEMIS.

Well yes – and if this were a rational woman
she would have stopped to think before she spoke.
She is, unfortunately, mad.
Tell me, what in the world do you have in mind

as you throw on your armour
and call me to your side?
Look at yourself! You are female, 1310
not male – born that way.
And you're no match for them in strength or in luck.
They are flush with fortune;
our luck has trickled away.
Really, Elektra,
who would think to topple a man of his stature?
Who could ever get away with it?
Be careful: this sort of blundering
might make things worse for us –
what if someone overhears! 1320
And there is nothing whatever to win or to gain
if we make ourselves famous and die in disgrace.
Death itself is not the worst thing.
Worse is to live
when you want to die.
So I beg you,
before you destroy us
and wipe out the family altogether,
control your temper.
As for your words, 1330
I will keep them secret – for your sake.
Oh Elektra, get some sense! It is almost too late.
Your strength is nothing,

you cannot beat them: give up.

CHORUS.
Hear that? Foresight! –
no greater asset a person can have
than foresight combined with good sense.

ELEKTRA.
Predictable.
I knew you'd say no.
Well: 1340
alone then.

One hand will have to be enough.
One hand *is* enough.

Yes.

CHRYSOTHEMIS.
Too bad you weren't so resolved
on the day Father died.
You could have finished the task.

ELEKTRA.
Yes, I had the guts for it then, but no strategy.

CHRYSOTHEMIS.
Forget strategy – you'll live longer.

ELEKTRA.
I gather you don't intend to help. 1350

CHRYSOTHEMIS.
Too risky for me.

ELEKTRA.
You have your own strategy, I see.
I admire that.

But your cowardice appalls me.

CHRYSOTHEMIS.
One day you will say I was right.

ELEKTRA.
Never.

CHRYSOTHEMIS.
The future will judge.

ELEKTRA.
Oh go away. You give no help.

CHRYSOTHEMIS.
You take no advice.

ELEKTRA.
Why not run off and tell all this to Mother? 1360

CHRYSOTHEMIS.
> I don't hate you that much.

ELEKTRA.
> At least realise you are driving me into dishonour.

CHRYSOTHEMIS.
> Dishonour? No: foresight.

ELEKTRA.
> And I should conform to your version of justice?

CHRYSOTHEMIS.
> When you are sane, you can think for us both.

ELEKTRA.
> Terrible to sound so right and be so wrong.

CHRYSOTHEMIS.
> Well put! You describe yourself to a fault.

ELEKTRA.
> Do you deny that I speak for justice?

CHRYSOTHEMIS.
> Let's just say there are times
> when justice is too big a risk. 1370

ELEKTRA.
> I will not live by rules like those.

CHRYSOTHEMIS.
> Go ahead then. You'll find out I was right.

ELEKTRA.
> I *do* go ahead. You cannot deter me.

CHRYSOTHEMIS.
> So you won't change your plan?

ELEKTRA.
> Immorality isn't a plan. It is the enemy.

CHRYSOTHEMIS.
> You don't hear a single word I say.

ELEKTRA.
Oh it was all decided long ago.

CHRYSOTHEMIS.
Well I'll be off.
It's clear you could never bring yourself
to praise my words, nor I your ways. 1380

ELEKTRA.
Yes. You do that. You be off.
But I will not follow you,
no.
Never.
Not even if you beg me.
When
I look in your eyes I see emptiness.

CHRYSOTHEMIS.
If that is your attitude,
that is your attitude.
When you're in deep trouble, 1390
you'll say I was right.

Exit CHRYSOTHEMIS.

CHORUS.
Why is it – *strophe 1*
we look at birds in the air,
we see it makes sense
the way they care
for the life of those who sow and sustain them –
why
is it
we don't do the same?
No: 1400
by lightning of Zeus,
by Themis of heaven,
not long

free of pain!
O
sound going down

to the dead in the
ground,
take a voice
take my voice, 1410
take down
pity
below
to Arteus' dead:
tell them shame.
Tell them there is no dancing.

Because *antistrophe 1*
here is a house falling sick
falling now
between two children battling, 1420
and there is no more level of love in the days.
Betrayed,
alone
she goes down in the waves:
Elektra,
grieving for death,
for her father,
as a nightingale
grieving always.
Nor 1430
does she think
to fear dying,
no!
she is glad
to go dark.
As a
killer
of furies,
as a pureblooded
child 1440
of the father who sowed her.
No one well-born *strophe 2*
is willing to live

with evil,
with shame,
with a name made nameless.
O child,
child,
you made your life a wall of tears
against dishonour: 1450
you fought and you won.
For they call you
the child of his mind,

child of his excellence.
I pray you raise your hand *antistrophe 2*
and crush the ones
who now
crush you!
For I see you subsisting
in mean part, 1460
and yet
you are one who kept faith
with the living laws,
kept faith
in the clear reverence
of Zeus.

Enter ORESTES *and* SERVANT *with urn.*

ORESTES.
Tell me ladies, did we get the right directions?
Are we on the right road? Is this the place?

CHORUS.
What place? What do you want?

ORESTES.
The place where Aegisthus lives. 1470

CHORUS.
Well here you are. Your directions were good.

ORESTES.
>   Which one of you, then, will tell those within?
>   Our arrival will please them.

CHORUS.
>   Her – as nearest of kin, she is the right one to
>   announce you.

ORESTES.
>   Please, my lady, go in and tell them
>   that certain Phocians are asking for Aegisthus.

ELEKTRA.
>   OIMOI TALAIN'.
>   Oh no. Don't say that. Don't say you have come with
>   evidence of the stories we heard. 1480

ORESTES.
>   I don't know what you heard.
>   Old Strophius sent me with news of Orestes.

ELEKTRA.
>   Oh stranger, what news? Fear comes walking into me.

ORESTES.
>   We have his remains in a small urn here –
>   for he's dead, as you see.

ELEKTRA.
>   OI 'GO TALAINA
>   Oh no. No. Not this thing in your hands.
>   No.

ORESTES.
>   If you have tears to shed for Orestes,
>   this urn is all that holds his body now. 1490

ELEKTRA.
>   Oh stranger, allow me, in god's name –
>   if this vessel does really contain him,
>   to hold it in my hands.
>   For myself, for the whole generation of us,

I have tears to keep,
I have ashes to weep.

ORESTES (*to* SERVANT *with urn*).
Bring it here, give it to her, whoever
she is.
It is no enemy asking this.
She is someone who loved him,
or one of his blood.

ELEKTRA.
If this were all you were, Orestes,
how could your memory
fill my memory,
how is it your soul fills my soul?
I sent you out, I get you back:
tell me
how could the difference be simply
nothing?
Look!
You are nothing at all.
Just a crack where the light slipped through.
Oh my child,
I thought I could save you.
I thought I could send you beyond.
But there is no beyond.
You might as well have stayed that day
to share your father's tomb.
Instead, somewhere, I don't know where –
suddenly alone you stopped –
where death was.
You stopped.
And I would have waited
and washed you
and lifted you
up from the fire,
like a whitened coal.
Strangers are so careless!
Look how you got smaller, coming back.
OIMOI TALAINA.

All my love   1530
gone for nothing.
Days of my love, years of my love.
Into your child's finger I put the earth and the sky.
No mother did that for you.
No nurse.
No slave.
I. Your sister
without letting go,
day after day, year after year,
and you my own sweet child.   1540

But death was a wind too strong for that.

One day three people vanished.
Father. You. Me. Gone.
Now our enemies rock with laughter.
And she runs mad for joy –
that creature
in the shape of your mother –
how often you said you would come
one secret evening and cut her throat!
But our luck cancelled that,   1550
whatever luck is.
And instead my beloved,
luck sent you back to me
colder than ashes,
later than shadow.
OIMOI MOI.
Pity,
PHEU PHEU
oh beloved,
OIMOI MOI
as you vanish down that road.   1560
Oh my love,
take me there.
Let me dwell where you are.
I am already nothing.
I am already burning.
Oh my love, I was once part of you –

take me too!
Only void is between us.
And I see that the dead feel no pain. 1570

CHORUS.
Elektra, be reasonable.
Your father was a mortal human being.
Orestes too – we all pay the same price for that.
Control yourself.

ORESTES.
PHEU PHEU.
What should I say? This is
impossible! I cannot hold my tongue much longer.

ELEKTRA.
What is the matter? What are you trying to say?

CHORUS.
Is this the brilliant Elektra?

ELEKTRA.
This is Elektra. Brilliant no more. 1580

ORESTES.
OIMOI TALAINES.
It hurts me to look at you.

ELEKTRA.
Surely, stranger, you're not feeling sorry for me?

ORESTES.
It shocks me, the way you look: do they abuse you?

ELEKTRA.
Yes, in fact. But who are you?

ORESTES.
PHEU.
What an ugly, loveless life for a girl.

ELEKTRA.
Why do you stare at me? Why are you so sympathetic?

ORESTES.
    I had no idea how bad my situation really is.

ELEKTRA.
    And what makes you realise that? Something I said?

ORESTES.
    Just to see the outline of your suffering.   1590

ELEKTRA.
    Yet this is only a fraction of it you see.

ORESTES.
    What could be worse than this?

ELEKTRA.
    To live in the same house with killers.

ORESTES.
    What killers? What evil are you hinting at?

ELEKTRA.
    My own father's killers.
    And I serve than as a slave. By compulsion.

ORESTES.
    Who compels you?

ELEKTRA.
    Mother she is called. Mother she is not.

ORESTES.
    How do you mean? Does she strike you? Insult you?

ELEKTRA.
    Yes. And worse.   1600

ORESTES.
    But you have no one to protect you?
    No one to stand in her way?

ELEKTRA.
    No. There was someone. Here are his ashes.

ORESTES.
    Oh girl. How I pity the dark life you live.

ELEKTRA.
No one else has ever pitied me, you know.

ORESTES.
No one else has ever been part of your grief.

ELEKTRA.
Do you mean you are somehow part of my family?

ORESTES.
I'll explain – if these women are trustworthy.

ELEKTRA.
Oh yes, you can trust them. Speak freely.

ORESTES.
Give back the urn, then, and you will hear everything. 1610

ELEKTRA.
No! Don't take this from me, for god's sake,
whoever you are!

ORESTES.
Come now, do as I say. It is the right thing.

ELEKTRA.
No! In all reverence no please – don't take this away.
It is all that I love.

ORESTES.
I forbid you to keep it.

ELEKTRA.
O TALAIN'EGO SETHEN.
Orestes! What if
they take from me
even the rites of your death! 1620

ORESTES.
Hush, now. That language is wrong.

ELEKTRA.
Wrong to mourn my own dead brother?

ORESTES.
Wrong for you to say that word.

ELEKTRA.
How did I lose the right to call him brother?

ORESTES.
Your rights you have. Your brother you don't.

ELEKTRA.
Do I not stand here with Orestes himself in my hands?

ORESTES.
No, in fact. That Orestes is a lie.

ELEKTRA.
Then where in the world is the poor boy's grave?

ORESTES.
Nowhere. The living need no grave.

ELEKTRA.
Child, what are you saying? 1630

ORESTES.
Nothing but the truth.

ELEKTRA.
The man is alive?

ORESTES.
As I live and breathe.

ELEKTRA.
You – ?

ORESTES.
Look at this ring – our father's –

ELEKTRA.
Father's!

ORESTES.
– and see what I mean.

ELEKTRA.
Oh love, you break on me like light!

ORESTES.
Yes like light!

ELEKTRA.
Oh voice, have you come out of nowhere? 1640

ORESTES.
Nowhere but where you are.

ELEKTRA.
Do I hold you now in my hands?

ORESTES.
Now and forever.

ELEKTRA.
Ladies, my friends, my people, look!
Here stands Orestes:
dead by device
now by device brought back to life!

ORESTES.
I see, child. And at this reversal,
my tears are falling for joy.

ELEKTRA.
IO GONAI. *strophe* 1650
You exist!
You came back,
you found me –

ORESTES.
Yes, I am here. Now keep silent a while.

ELEKTRA.
Why?

ORESTES.
Silence is better. Someone inside might overhear.

ELEKTRA.
By Artemis unbroken! I would not

dignify with fear
the dull surplus of females
who huddle in that house!

ORESTES.
Careful! There is war in women too,
as you know by experience, I think.

ELEKTRA.
OTOTOTOTOI TOTOI.
You drive me back down my desperation –
that unclouded

incurable
never forgotten
evil
growing inside my life.

ORESTES.
I know, but we should talk of those deeds
when the moment is right.

ELEKTRA.
Every arriving moment of my life *antistrophe*
has a right
to tell those deeds!
And this chance to speak freely is hard won.

ORESTES.
Precisely. Safeguard it.

ELEKTRA.
How?

ORESTES.
When the time is unsuitable, no long speeches.

ELEKTRA.
But how could silence be the right way to greet
you – simply
coming
out of nowhere
like a miracle?

ORESTES.
It was a miracle set in motion by the gods.

ELEKTRA.
Ah.

That is a vast claim
and much more beautiful,
to think
some god
has brought you here.   1690
Some god: yes! That must be true.

ORESTES.
Elektra, I do not like to curb your rejoicing
but I am afraid when you lose control.

ELEKTRA.
Oh but my love –
now that you have travelled back down all those years

to meet my heart,
over all this grief of mine,
do not
oh love –

ORESTES.
What are you asking?   1700

ELEKTRA.
Do not turn your face from me.
Don't take yourself away.

ORESTES.
Of course not. No one else will take me either.

ELEKTRA.
Do you mean that?

ORESTES.
Yes I do.

ELEKTRA.
Oh beloved,

ELEKTRA 65

    I heard your voice
    when I had no hope
    and my heart leapt away from me
    calling   1710
    you.
    I was in sorrow.
    But now
    I am holding you,
    now you are visible –
    light of the face I could never forget.

ORESTES.
    Spare me these words.
    You don't need to teach me my mother is evil
    or how Aegisthus drains the family wealth,
    pours it out like water,   1720
    sows it to the wind.
    We've no time for all that – talk is expensive.
    What I need now are the practical details:
    where we should hide, where we can leap out
    and push that enemy laughter
    right back down their throats!
    But be careful she doesn't read
    the fact of our presence
    straight from the glow on your face.
    You must keep on lamenting   1730
    my fictitious death.
    Time enough
    for lyres and laughter
    when we've won the day.

ELEKTRA.
    Your will and my will are one: identical, brother.
    For I take all my joy from you,
    none is my own.
    Nor could I harm you ever so slightly
    at any price: it would be a disservice
    to the god who stands beside us now.   1740
    So. You know what comes next.
    Aegisthus has gone out,

Mother is home.
And don't worry:
she'll see no glow on my face.
Hatred put out the light in me a long time ago.
Besides, since I saw you
my tears keep running down –
tears, joy, tears all mixed up together.
How could I stop? 1750
I saw you come down that road a dead man,
I looked again and saw you alive.
You have used me strangely.
Why – if Father suddenly came back to life
I wouldn't call it fantastic.

Believe what you see.
But
now you have come,
I am yours to command. 1760
Alone,
I would have done one of two things:
deliver myself or else die.

ORESTES.
Quiet! I hear someone coming out.

ELEKTRA.
Go inside, strangers.
You are bringing a gift
they can neither reject nor rejoice in.

Enter OLD MAN.

OLD MAN.
Idiots! Have you lost your wits completely,
and your instinct to survive as well –
or were you born brainless?
You're not on the brink of disaster now, 1770
you're right in the eye of it, don't you see that?
Why, except for me standing guard at the door here
this long while, your plans
would have been in the house

before yourselves!
Good thing I took caution.
Now cut short the speechmaking,
stifle your joy
and go in the house. Go!
Delay is disaster in things like this. 1780
Get it over with: that's the point now.

ORESTES.
How will I find things inside?

OLD MAN.
Perfect. No one will know you.

ORESTES.
You reported me dead?

OLD MAN.
You are deep in hell, so far as they know.

ORESTES.
Are they happy at this?

OLD MAN.
I'll tell you that later. For now,
the whole plan is unfolding beautifully.
Even the ugly parts.

ELEKTRA.
Who is this man, brother? 1790

ORESTES.
Don't you know him?

ELEKTRA.
Not even remotely.

ORESTES.
You don't know the man into whose hands you put me,
once long ago?

ELEKTRA.
What man? What are you saying?

ORESTES.
 The man who smuggled me off to Phocia,
 thanks to your foresight.

ELEKTRA.
 Him? Can it be? That man was
 the one trustworthy soul I could find in the house,
 the day Father died! 1800

ORESTES.
 That's who he is. Do not question me further.

ELEKTRA (*to the* OLD MAN).
 I bless you like the light of day!
 I bless you
 as the saviour of the house of Agamemnon!
 How did you come? Is it really you –
 who pulled us up from the pit that day?
 I bless your hands,
 I bless your feet,
 I bless the sweet roads you walked!
 How strange 1810
 you were beside me all that time and gave no sign.
 Strange – to destroy me with lies
 when you had such sweet truth to tell.
 Bless you, Father! – Yes, Father.
 That is who I see when I look at you now.

 There is no man on earth I have hated and loved like you
 on the one same day.

OLD MAN.
 Enough, now. As for all the stories in between –
 there will be nights and days
 to unravel them, Elektra. 1820
 But for you two, standing here,
 I have just one word: act!
 Now is the moment!
 Now Clytemnestra is alone.
 Now there is not one man in the house.

If you wait you will have to fight others,
more skilled and more numerous. Think!

ORESTES.
Well, Pylades, no more speeches.
As quick as we can
into the house – after 1830
we pay our respects
to the gods of this doorway.

Exit ORESTES *and* PYLADES *followed by the* OLD MAN.

ELEKTRA.
King Apollo! Graciously hear them
Hear me too! I have been devout,
I have come to you often,

bringing you gifts of whatever I had.
Now again I come with all that I have:
Apollo wolfkiller! I beg you!
I call out –
I fall to my knees! 1840
Please send your mind over us,
inform our strategies,
show
how the gods reward
unholy action!

CHORUS.
Look where he comes grazing forward, *strophe*
blood bubbling over his lips: Ares!
As a horizontal scream into the house
go the hunters of evil,
the raw and deadly dogs. 1850
Not long now:
the blazing dream of my head is crawling out.

Here he comes like a stealing shadow, *antistrophe*
like a footprint of death into the rooms,
stalking the past

with freshcut blood in his hands.
It is Hermes who guides him
down a blindfold of shadow –
straight to finish line: not long now!

ELEKTRA.
My ladies! The men
are about to accomplish the deed –
be silent and wait.

CHORUS.
How? What are they doing?

ELEKTRA.
She is dressing the urn. They are standing beside her.

CHORUS.
But why did you come running out here?

ELEKTRA.
To watch that Aegusthus doesn't surprise is.

CLYTEMNESTRA (*within*).
AIAI IO.
Rooms
filled with murder!

ELEKTRA.
Someone inside screams – do you hear?

CHORUS.
Yes I hear. It makes my skin crawl.

CLYTEMNESTRA.
OIMOI TALAIN'.
Aegisthus, where are you?

ELEKTRA.
There! Again! Someone calls out.

CLYTEMNESTRA.
Oh child my child, pity the mother who bore you!

ELEKTRA.
> Yet you had little enough pity for him
> and none for his father!

CHORUS.
> Alas for the city.
> Alas for a whole race thrown and shattered:
> the shape that followed you down the days
> is dying now, dying away.

CLYTEMNESTRA.
> OMOI.
> I am hit!

ELEKTRA.
> Hit her a second time, if you have the strength!

CLYTEMNESTRA.
> OMOI MAL' AUTHIS.
> Again!

ELEKTRA.
> If only Aegisthus could share this!

CHORUS.
> The curses are working.
> Under the ground
> dead men are alive
> with their black lips moving,
> black mouths sucking
> on the soles of killer's feet.
>
> Here they come,
> hands soaked with red: Ares is happy!
> Enough said.

ELEKTRA.
> Orestes, how does it go?

ORESTES.
> Good, so far – at least so far as Apollo's oracle was
> good.

ELEKTRA.
Is the creature dead? 1900

ORESTES.
Your good mother will not insult you any more.

CHORUS.
Stop! I see Aegisthus coming yes, it is him.

ELEKTRA.
Children, get back!

ORESTES.
Where do you see him –

ELEKTRA.
There – marching right down on us
full of joy.

CHORUS.
Go quick to the place just inside the front door.
You have won the first round. Now for the second.

ORESTES.
Don't worry. We will finish this.

ELEKTRA.
Hurry. Go to it. 1910

ORESTES.
Yes I am gone.

ELEKTRA.
And leave this part to me.

CHORUS.
Why not drop a few friendly words in his ear –
so his moment of justice may come
as a surprise.

Enter AEGISTHUS.

AEGISTHUS.
Does anyone know where those Phocian strangers are?
People say they have news of Orestes

dead in a chariot crash.
You!
yes you! – you've never been shy 1920
to speak your mind
And obviously this matter most concerns you.

ELEKTRA.
Yes of course I know, for I do keep track
of the fortunes of the family.

AEGISTHUS.
Where are they then,
the strangers? – tell me.

ELEKTRA.
Inside the house, for they've fallen upon
the perfect hostess.

AEGISTHUS.
And it's true they bring a report of his death?

ELEKTRA.
No – better: they have evidence, 1930
not just words.

AEGISTHUS.
We can see proof?

ELEKTRA.
You can, indeed, though it's no pretty sight.

AEGISTHUS.
Well this is good news. Unusual, coming from you.

ELEKTRA.
Relish it while you can.

AEGISTHUS.
Silence! I say throw open the gates!
for every Mycenaean and Argive to see –
in case you had placed empty hopes
in this man –
take my bit on your tongue 1940
or learn the hard way.

ELEKTRA.
As for me, I am playing my part to the end.
I've learned to side with the winners.

> *A shrouded corpse is disclosed with* ORESTES
> *and* PYLADES *standing beside it.*

AEGISTHUS.
O Zeus! I see here a man fallen by the jealousy of god
– but
if that remark offends,
I unsay it.

Uncover the eyes. Uncover it all.
I should pay my respects.

ORESTES.
Uncover it yourself.   1950
This isn't my corpse – it's yours.
Yours to look at, yours to eulogise.

AEGISTHUS.
Yes good point. I have to agree.
You there – Clytemnestra must be about in the house –
call her for me.

ORESTES.
She is right here before you. No need to look elsewhere.

AEGISTHUS.
OIMOI.
What do I see!

ORESTES.
You don't know the face?

AEGISTHUS.
Caught! But *who set the trap*?   1960

ORESTES.
Don't you realise yet
that you're talking to dead men alive?

AEGISTHUS.
   OIMOI.
   I do understand. You are Orestes.

ORESTES.
   At last.

AEGISTHUS.
   I'm a dead man. No way out.
   But let me just say –

ELEKTRA.
   No!
   Don't let him speak –
   by the gods! Brother – no speechmaking now!   1970
   When a human being is so steeped in evil as this one
   what is gained by delaying his death?
   Kill him at once.
   Throw his corpse out
   for scavengers to get.
   Nothing less than this
   can cut the knot of evils
   inside me.

ORESTES.
   Get in with you, quickly
   This is no word game: 1980
   your life is at stake.

AEGISTHUS.
   Why take me inside?
   If the deed is honourable, what need of darkness?
   You aren't ready to kill?

ORESTES.
   Don't give me instructions, just get yourself in:
   You will die on the spot
   where you slaughtered my father.

AEGISTHUS.
   Must these rooms see

the whole evil of Pelops' race,
present and future? 1990

ORESTES.
They will see yours, I can prophesy.

AEGISTHUS.
That is no skill you got from your father!

ORESTES.
Your answers are quick, your progress slow.
Go.

AEGISTHUS.
You lead the way.

ORESTES.
No you go first.

AEGISTHUS.
Afraid I'll escape?

ORESTES.
You shall not die on your own terms.
I will make it bitter for you.
And let such judgement fall 2000
on any who wish to break the law:
kill them!
The evil were less.

Exit ORESTES *and* AEGISTHUS,
followed by ELEKTRA, *into the house.*

CHORUS.
O seed of Atreus:
you suffered and broke free,

you took aim and struck;
you have won your way through
to the finish.

Exit CHORUS.

Afterword
Screaming in Translation: The *Elektra* of Sophokles
Anne Carson

> *And how the red wild sparkles dimly burn*
> *Through the ashen grayness.*

Elizabeth Barrett Browning

A translator is someone trying to get in between a body and its shadow. Translating is a task of imitation that faces in two directions at once, for it must line itself up with the solid body of the original text and at the same time with the shadow of that text where it falls across another language. Shadows fall and move. The following paper, based on my own attempts to render the Greek text of Sophokles' *Elektra* into English, will indicate some of the moving shadows cast by this unusual and difficult play and describe how they have proven problematic for its translation into readable verse and performable drama.[1]

First I will consider screaming. Because the presence in Greek drama of bursts of sound expressing strong emotion (like OIMOI or O TALAINA or PHEU PHEU) furnishes the translator with a very simple and intractable problem. It has been generally assumed that they represent a somewhat formulaic body of ejaculatory utterance best rendered into English by some dead phrase like Alas! or Woe is me! But I discovered when studying the language of Elektra that her screams are far from formulaic. They contribute to her characterisation as creatively as many other aspects of her diction.

---

1. I am grateful to Francis Dunn (then) of Northwestern University in Chicago (now UC Santa Barbara), who gave me the opportunity to present this paper at the symposium *Sophocles' Electra: Greek Tragedy In Word and Action* cosponsored by the Departments of Classics and Theatre in May 1993. Greek texts are cited from the edition of Sir Richard Jebb, Cambridge, 1894. Works consulted include the translation of D. Grene in *Sophocles II*, Chicago, 1957, the commentar of J. C. Kamerbeek, Leiden, 1974, the edition of R. H. Mather 1889, and the translation of Ezra Pound and R. Flemming, New York, 1990.

Elektra's diction, especially her verbs, is the second topic I will discuss. There is one particular verb, repeated seven times in the play, with which Sophokles takes linguistic risks that have no synonym in English. It is a verb that means 'to cause pain' and Elektra uses it in unique ways. The uniqueness of Elektra's pain emerges not only from her diction but also musically. Thirdly and very briefly I will discuss the verbal and rhythmic music of Elektra, especially in her interactions with the chorus in the opening movement of the play.

Screaming is a fairly typical activity of characters in Greek drama. But it was Virginia Woolf who noticed, perhaps after a night of listening to the birds in her garden talking ancient Greek, that there is something original about the screaming of Sophokles' Elektra. In her essay on this play in *The Common Reader* Virginia Woolf says:[2]

> ...his Elektra stands before us like a figure so tightly bound that she can only move an inch this way, an inch that. But each movement must tell to the utmost, or... she will be nothing but a dummy, tightly bound. Her words in crisis are, as a matter of fact, bare; mere cries of despair, joy, hate... But it is not so easy to decide what it is that gives these cries of Elektra in her anguish their power to cut and wound and excite.

Indeed it is not easy to decide what gives the screaming of Elektra its power. Sophokles has invented for her a language of lament that is like listening to an X-ray. Elektra's cries are just bones of sound. I itemise the cries of Elektra as follows:

1. O
2. IO
3. PHEU
4. AIAI
5. OIMOI MOI
6. IO MOI MOI
7. EE IO
8. EE IO
9. EE AIAI
10. IO GONAI
11. OIMOI TALAINA

2. London. 1925. p. 26.

12. OI 'GO TALAINA
13. OTOTOTOTOI TO TOI
14. IO MOI MOI DYSTENOS

In range and diversity of aural construction Elektra surpasses all other screamers in Sophokles, including Philoctetes who suffers from gangrene in the foot and Heracles who gets burned alive at the end of his play. Let us consider how Elektra constructs her screams. It should be noted at the outset that none of them occur extra metrum: they scan, and are to be taken as integral to the rhythmic and musical economy of her utterance. As units of sound they employ the usual features of ritual lament (assonance, alliteration, internal rhyme, balance, symmetry, repetition)[3] in unusual ways. She creates, for example, certain unpronounceable concatenations of hiatus like EE AIAI or EE IO which hold the voice and the mouth open for the whole length of a measure of verse and are as painful to listen to as they are to say. The effect of such sounds is well described by Elektra herself at 242–3, where she refers to her own language of lament in the phrase:

pterygas / oxytonôn goôn
πτέρυγας / ὀξυτόνων γόων

literally, 'wings of sharpstretched laments' or 'wings of screamings that are strained to sharp points'. The phrase in Greek undulates harshlv, onomatopoeic of the cries themselves. But it has also an image of straining or stretching – the straining of sound and emotion against enclosing limits – which is important to the concept of the whole passage. Elektra here is talking about the evil of the house of Atreus as if it were a trap that has closed around her life. She believes that nothing except her voice can penetrate the walls of this enclosure. 'My cries are wings, they pierce the cage' is how I translated the verse, losing the sound effect of the Greek but retaining the aggressivity of the cries and also the terrible sense of stuckness that characterises Elektra's self-descriptions. For example at v. 132f. she summarises her own stuck situation in the double negative construction:

---

[3]. On characteristics of funeral lament, see M. Alexiou, *The Ritual Lament in Greek Tradition*, Cambridge, 1974.

oud' ethelô… / mê ou… stenachein
οὐδ ἐθέλω… / μὴ οὐ… στενάχειν
'I cannot *not* grieve…'

This same stuckness informs certain of the screams of Elektra, for example the strangely compressed *oi 'go talaina*. This phrase is a three-part construction which combines the exclamation *oi* (conventionally translated 'Alas!' or the like) with the first-person singular pronoun *egô* ('I') and the standard adjective of tragic self-description *talaina* ('wretched, pitiable, miserable, sorry, sad, messed-up'). These three components are forced together at high emotional pressure as if they formed a single entity of sound and self. It is an entity that elides Elektra of part of her *egô*: the pronoun *egô* sacrifices its opening vowel to the encroachment of the exclamatory *oi* and then merges immediately with the epithet *talaina* so as to enclose Elektra's *egô* in grief from both sides. As she says of herself at v. 147 'Grieving is a pattern that is cut and fitted around my mind' (*eme… araren phrenas*).

The mind of Elektra is a remarkable machinery. It provides an unrelentingly lucid commentary on her stuck situation from the first moment she enters the stage. She begins the parodos, for example, by naming two other stuck people as paradigms for herself, Niobe who is literally petrified by grief for her dead children, and Procne who has been transformed into a nightingale by remorse for her dead son. But it is not their emotional paralysis that Elektra venerates. For her, Niobe and Procne represent a victory of female sign language. They are women who have left behind human form and rational speech yet have not let go the making of meaning. The water that pours perpetually down Niobe's rock face, the twittering that pours perpetually from Procne's bird mouth, are analogues for Elektra's private language of screams. Each of these three women manages to say what she means from within an idiolect that is alien or unknown to other people. Each of them manages, although stuck in a form of life that cuts her off from the world of normal converse, to transect and trouble and change that world by her utterance. Elektra admires Niobe and Procne because each of them has a significatory power, as she does, herself, to sabotage the world of other people and normal converse.

Now Elektra has a special verb for this action of sabotage, which she has come to regard as identical with her own function. It is the verb *lupein* and it figures in one of the strangest sentences of the play. The Greek lexicon defines *lupein* in the active as 'to grieve, vex, cause pain, do harm, harass, distress, damage, violate' and in the passive as 'to be vexed, violated, harassed', etc., or 'to grieve, feel pain'. The cognate noun *lupe* means 'pain of body' or 'pain of mind' or 'sad plight.' Elektra uses this verb to assert her philosophy of action at v. 355, where she says that public lament is her whole function in life because by this action she can *lupein* – grieve, harass, distress, damage, violate – her mother. In the following verses she summarises her philosophy of self in a sentence formed around this same verb *lupein*:

> emoi gar estô toume mê lupein monon / boskêma (363–4)
> ἐμοὶ γὰρ ἔστω τοὐμὲ μὴ λυπεῖν μόνον / βόσκημα
> ['For me yes let be not damaging me the only food.']

> 'For me be it food enough that I do not wound mine own conscience.' (R. C. Jebb)

> 'For me let it be meat and drink not to put my self out.' (R. H. Mather)

> 'All the food I need is the quiet of my conscience.' (D. Grene)

> 'Keep my self-respect anyhow.' (E. Pound)

During the days and weeks when I was working on this play I used to dream about translating. One night I dreamed that the text of the play was a big solid glass house. I floated above the house trying to zero in on v. 363. I was carrying in my hands wrapped in a piece of black cloth the perfect English equivalent for *lupein* and I kept trying to force myself down through the glass atmosphere of the house to position this word in its right place. But there was an upward pressure as heavy as water. I couldn't move down, I swam helplessly back and forth on the surface of the transparency, waving my black object and staring down at the text through fathoms of glass. And I was just about to take the black cloth off and look at the word so as to memorise it for later when I awoke, when I awoke.

I never did discover, asleep or awake, what was under that black cloth. I never did hit upon the right translation for *lupein*. But Elektra's use of this verb (particularly at v. 363) continues to disturb me because of the way it sums her up. As Virginia Woolf says, 'the stable, the permanent, the original human being is to be found there.'[4] When we look at the syntax of v. 363 we see a sentence formed around a verb, the infinitive *lupein*, but the verb is made into a negative by the addition of the adverb *me* ('to not vex, harm, damage, etc.') and then the negatived verb is made into a noun by the addition of the article *to* ('the act of not vexing, harming, damaging, etc.'). So too in Elektra's life we see all positive action negated by hatred and then this negative condition reified as personal destiny. Actionless, she feeds on her own negativity. 'It is the only Food that grows,' as Emily Dickinson says of another equally private religion of pain.[5] This strange black food is named again by Elektra, this time as a noun, at v. 822 in its full suicidal implication:

> lupê d' ean zô· tou biou d' oudeis pothos.
> λύπη δ' ἐὰν ζῶ τοῦ βίου δ' οὐδεὶς πόθος.
> 'It is damage [pain, violation, etc.] if I continue to exist.
>   No desire for life [is in me].'

She expresses another death wish with the participle of the verb at v. 1170:

> tous gar thanontas oukh horô lupoumenous.
> τοὺς γὰρ θανόντας οὐχ ὁρῶ λυπουμένους,
> 'For the dead, I see, feel no pain.'

Elektra has a talent for brutal antithesis but these statements are not, I think, rhetorically formed. They touch a null point at the centre of the woman's soul. And they have the same X-ray quality as some of her screams.

But for the translator the problem presented by Elektra's screams and diction in general is contextual. She uses fairly common verbs and nouns, and Sophokles goes out of his way to show us her X-ray utterances projected on the ordinary language screen of other people. This creates an especially

---

4. *The Common Reader* [n. 2, above].
5. T. H. Johnson, ed., *The Complete Poems of Emily Dickinson*, Boston, 1890, #1555.

jarring effect when we hear them using her words. For example when Orestes, dismissing the notion that lying and deceit are bad things, tosses off the phrase:

> ti gar me lupei touth'…
> τί γάρ με λυπεῖ τοῦθ'…
> 'What harm does this do me [to die in words if I am saved in fact]?' (50–60)

In Orestes' much more lightly maintained moral order, Elektra's black verb *lupei* is little more than a synonym for 'What's the problem?' A similar shock effect is felt when we hear Clytemnestra appropriate Elektra's noun *lupê* to denote pain of childbirth. Clytemnestra is referring to Agamemnon and Iphigeneia when she says (532–33),

> …ouk ison kamôn emoi / lupês, hot' espeir', hôsper hê tiktous' egô.
> …οὐκ ἴσον καμὼν ἐμοὶ / λύπης, ὅτ' ἔσπειρ', ὥσπερ ἡ τίκτουσ' ἐγώ.
> '…Did he have some share in the pain [*lupês*] of her birth? No! I did it myself.'

This is one category of pain that the resolutely asexual Elektra will never know, and furthermore, as she tells us repeatedly throughout the play, the very idea of genetic connexion or genital analogy between herself and her mother fills her with horror. 'Mother she is called but mother she is not,' Elektra announces at one point to her sister. And although on one level Elektra can be said to instantiate every girl's fear of turning into her mother, it is also true that in this case both the girl and the mother are prodigious – the mother for her shamelessness, the girl for her shame. It is not until we hear Clytemnestra decline Elektra's word *lupê* to its most fleshly and female connotation that we understand Elektra's shame in its full human and sexual aspect. There is something *unnatural*, something radical and alien, for Sophokles and his audience, about the way female shame has constructed around Elektra a sort of life-size funeral urn which she inhabits as if it were a life.

Alienation is also indicated musically in the Sophoklean text. Elektra's music is a standing discrepancy to tragic convention and other people's expectations. She takes over the stage musically from the first moment of her entrance – in fact from before her entrance, for the first sound Elektra makes at v. 77 interrupts the iambic procedure of the prologue with an offstage scream in what seems an aborted lyric anapaest. The monodic song of Elektra that follows is intrusive in every way. It replaces the entrance song of the chorus which should occur at this point and usurps the anapaestic metre in which the chorus conventionally sing the entrance song. Rhetorically, Elektra's monody rivals anything in Greek drama for the sheer egotism of its address. She begins by saying (86–87):

ô phaos hagnon / kai gês isomoir' aêr...
ὦ φάος ἁγνὸν / καὶ γῆς ἰσόμοιρ' ἀήρ...
'O holy light and equal air shaped on the world...'

and goes on to call the entire cosmos to collaborate in her private drama of mourning and revenge. But the odd thing about this cosmic song is that it both begins and ends with a metaphor of measure. In the first verse (87) she measures air against earth with the phrase *gês isomoir' aêr*, and in the last verse she measures herself against the whole history of evil in the house of Atreus saying (119–20),

mounê gar agein ouketi sôkô / lupês antirrhopon achthos.
μούνη γὰρ ἄγειν οὐκέτι σωκῶ / λύπης ἀντίρροπον ἄχθος.
'Because alone the whole poised force of my life is nothing against this pain.'

It is typical of Sophoklean heroes to set for themselves cosmic parameters of moral action. By framing Elektra in images of measure, Sophokles reminds us that she is someone off the scale. And he is able to make this heroic discrepancy clear, in the long lyric interchange between Elektra and the chorus that follows her monody, by a very simple musical effect.

The dramatic purpose of this interchange is to show Elektra in interaction with a society sympathetic to her dilemma and realistic about her options. And moreover to show Elektra, in the midst of such people, utterly alone. The antiphonal nature of the song emphasises this.

Antiphony organises the song into alternating strophes and antistrophes. Each strophic pair follows a principle of

responsion whereby the first verse of the strophe responds
metrically with the first verse of the antistrophe, the second
verse with the second verse, and so on. This arrangement is
generally used to create a lyric dialogue between two voices.
If Elektra and the chorus had sung strophe and antistrophe
respectively, the effect would have been one of shared thought
or interwoven emotion. But Sophokles has chosen to further
subdivide each strophe and antistrophe so that each six lines of
Elektra respond with another six lines of Elektra, each six lines
of the chorus respond with another six lines of the chorus. They
are each talking to themselves. Musically, it is an anti-dialogue.

Conceptually also. Each time the chorus talk they send a
drift of platitudes down over Elektra who knocks them away
with one hand. Each choral utterance attempts to steer the
discussion towards general truths and perspectives wider
than the individual life. Elektra keeps pulling the focus back
to herself with a resolute first-person pronoun or verb. The
chorus talk strategies for going on with life, Elektra declares
life an irrelevancy. It is death that absorbs Elektra's whole
imagination and the darkness that is soaking out of this one
fact seems to colour the music and reasoning of everything
she says in the song, especially when we see these continually
measured against the bright banalities of the chorus. And at the
point where Elektra's anger and despair finally boil over (236)
she throws the metaphor of measure back at the chorus with a
question as jagged as a scream:

> kai ti metron kakotâtos ephu?
> καὶ τί μέτρον κακότατος ἔφυ;
> 'And at what point does the evil level off in my life,
>   tell me that!'

Nobody answers her.

Notes on the Text
Michael Shaw

A few formal terms: The basic divisions of a Greek tragedy, according to the tradition, is into prologue, parodos, episodes, and stasima. A Greek tragedy contains a variety of levels of speech, in the most general terms the meter of spoken verse (iambic trimeters) and lyric. The prologue and the episodes are usually in iambic trimeter. Characters may speak to each other or to the chorus. A lyric exchange between the chorus and one or more characters is a *kommos*. The *parados* is the entry song of the chorus (in *Elektra* this takes the form of a *kommos* between Elektra and the chorus). A *stasimon* is a choral song that divides two *episodes*. The *episodes*, which are mostly in iambic trimeter, are what we would call scenes; the final *episode*, which ends the drama, can also be called the *exodos*. These choral songs are typically constructed of strophe, antistrophe, and epode. A strophe is a stanza, while an antistrophe is a stanza whose metrical form closely follows that of a strophe. An epode is a single stanza which follows a paired strophe and antistrophe, but whose metrical form is unique.

1–162   This prologue has two parts, a dialogue in iambics spoken by Orestes and the Old Man and a monody by Elektra. The Old Man is called Paedagogus here because he is the servant who raised Orestes.

Scene   *The door to the palace is in the background, and beside it stands a statue of Apollo.* ORESTES *and* PYLADES *are distinguished from the* OLD MAN *by their dress, since he is a servant.* ORESTES *and* PYLADES *are dressed as young men of nobility and are wearing travellers' hats.*

6   *The grove of Io…* This may not be a specific place, but rather it may refer to all of Argos. There are parallels between Orestes' story and that of Io, which is given in the Glossary.

88 ELEKTRA

7–9 *...the marketplace / named for Apollo, / wolfkiller god.* This Argive feature is not identified. See the Glossary for 'Apollo wolfkiller'.

10 *...the famous temple of Hera.* The Argive temple to Hera is approximately a mile south of Mycenae.

17 *From the hands of your sister.* Neither Aeschylus nor Euripides say that Elektra saved Orestes, and this is probably the invention of Sophokles.

107 *IO MOI MOI DYSTENOS.* This is a traditional cry of grief. '*Dystenos*' means wretched. Inarticulate or nearly inarticulate cries of grief, pain, sorrow, surprise, etc., are common in this play. See the Afterword.

115–62 Monody (sung verse); the meter changes in the Greek text from iambic trimeter to a lyric meter, in this case lyric anapests.

144 *nightingale.* See Philomela in the Glossary.

163–333 The *parodos* consists of a duet (*kommos*) between the chorus and Elektra.

199 *the bird who calls Itys!* Philomela again, here linked to Niobe (see Glossary).

282 *pain on pain to pay* This repeats the alliteration of *p* in the Greek line: *poinima pathea pathein poroi.*

334–647 In the first *episode*, Elektra begins with a monologue, and the rest of the scene is a dialogue between Elektra and Chrysothemis.

338 *I am ashamed...* In the Greek text, Elektra's first word is 'I am ashamed.' Perhaps there is a hint here that Elektra is the opposite of Clytemnestra, who said 'I am not ashamed' at the beginning of two major speeches in Aeschylus' *Agamemnon* (856 and 1373).

444 *Enter Chrysothemis* As we will soon hear, Chrysothemis is more richly dressed than Elektra, who is herself probably dressed as a servant. There is no embroidery on Elektra's 'belt', and thus we can assume that such embroidery is visible on Chrysothemis'

costume as it is on that of Clytemnestra. As a
noblewoman, Chrysothemis probably should have an
attendant, but she carries at least some of the offerings
in her own hands.

466 *not a word is your own…* Kells claims this charge is
not fair, but it seems accurate to me. Chrysothemis is
not simply in the wrong. By accepting the benefits of
a corrupt government, she shares responsibility for its
acts to some degree.

468 *sensible* This term (*phronein*) is prominent here, just
as it was in the dialogue of Antigone and Ismene in
Sophokles' *Antigone*. It can apply both to 'justice' and
to 'expediency'. Elektra ironically uses the word in its
expediency signification. Chrysothemis later ends her
speech with this word ('sensible,' 530).

543 *we have masters, we must bend* This is the language
of 'expediency'. Elektra counters with 'lick their
boots' – that is, Chrysothemis' position is one of
base flattery (*thopeia*). Chrysothemis counters with a
charge of stupidity (*aboulia*, 546). Prometheus uses
similar language in a similar situation in Aeschylus'
Prometheus Bound. He sneeringly urges the chorus to
'flatter' Zeus (*thopte*, 937). Hermes urges him to 'think
straight' (*eu phronein*, 1000). He accuses Prometheus
of preferring audacity to 'good thought' (*euboulia*,
1035).

586 *plain stupidity.* Chrysothemis ends her account of the
dream and returns to her earlier remarks, repeating the
word *stupidity* (*aboulia*) (see preceeding note).

648–91 In the first *stasimon*, the chorus reflect on
Clytemnestra's dream: justice will come.

663–69 *Vengeance… where marriage should never have
happened!* The Greek word for vengeance is *Erinys* (a
Fury). Once again, the chorus uses archaic language.
In the very difficult Greek of this passage, the marriage
of Clytemnestra and Aegisthus is said to be 'without a
bed, without a bride' (*alektra, anumpha*). The pun on

Elektra's name is probably intentional. The same pun appears in 1266–67 when Elektra tells Chrysothemis that she will grow old 'unbedded' (*alektra*) if Aegisthus and Clytemnestra remain in power. Thus the actions of Clytemnestra and Aegisthus have made their own marriage dysfunctional (i.e. their children have no inheritance rights, no status) and made marriage impossible for everyone else in the royal line. Elektra herself is only one embodiment of that frustration.

692–1391 The second *episode* begins with the entry of Clytemnestra, and the first part of the *episode* is a dialogue with Elektra. The Old Man then enters and gives his messenger speech, followed by comments by all three actors, after which Clytemnestra and the Old Man exit. Elektra remains and sings a *kommos* with the chorus. Chrysothemis enters; the sisters quarrel; Chrysothemis exits.

745 *...about the dead man and my sister as well* We need only examine the speech that follows to see that this is not spoken in complete candour. Elektra is an artful rhetorician as well as a passionate one.

755–67 *Ask Artemis... Hence, the sacrifice.* Aeschylus does not give a specific human action as the cause of Artemis' wrath at Aulis. Rather, the seer Calchas infers that wrath from an omen. Euripides more or less follows the version given here. These events are the subject of Euripides' *Iphigenia in Aulis.*

788 *You share... making children.* The Greek has a wonderful run of *p*'s here: 'palamnaioi, meth hou / patera ton amon prosthen exapolesas, / kai paidopoieis.' Elektra is literally spewing. The children of Clytemnestra and Aegisthus were Aletes and Erigone. There are references to plays by Sophokles with each of these names. (See Hyginus, *Fabula* 122 for stories about these children and Elektra and Orestes.)

816 *bitch* This word is not found in the Greek text, and there seems to be no hint here (as there is elsewhere) that Elektra is a 'dog' and hence a Fury. Rather, this

translation refers to the Greek word *shameless*, also a quality associated with dogs.

946–56 *Achaea... Boeotian* The competitors seem to be diverse in geography and in chronology. One is from Achaea, on the north coast of the Peloponnese, one is a Spartan from the central Peloponnese, two are from Libya (and thus strictly speaking postheroic); one is from Thessaly in north-eastern Greece, one is Aetolian, from west of Delphi, one is a Magnesian and one is an Aenian – both tribes in Thessaly mentioned in Homer; and one is a Boeotian and one is an Athenian.

990 *He had put his faith in the finish.* There may be some allegorical point in this detail. In Book 10 of the *Republic*, Plato has Socrates defend just action by saying that the just man finishes the race, while the unjust man is tripped up. Here Orestes does not seem to finish the race, but of course he will in fact do so.

1077 *Nemesis! Hear her!* Elektra appeals to the goddess of retribution to punish Clytemnestra for saying that her son Orestes is 'well off' being dead. Clytemnestra's reply probably refers to Orestes' death threats against her, for which Nemesis has punished him.

1092 *She went off laughing...* Here as often in Greek literature and in Sophokles, a person wronged imagines his or her enemies laughing.

1125 *Don't make that sound.* There is a very interesting scholium (an ancient or medieval note preserved in our manuscript tradition) on this line: 'It is necessary for the actor to look up to heaven as he makes this cry and to hold out his hands. The chorus restrains him by saying "Do not say anything excessive."'

1203 *Beloved Orestes.* In a play full of expressions of love, this is the most extreme: 'most beloved of all mortals'.

1204 *I said not a word.* Literally, 'I did not utter a word of ill omen.' Jebb assumes she refrained from reproaching Orestes for coming too late. He rejects the view that a cry of joy would be ill-omened at her father's tomb.

92 ELEKTRA

> I believe the remote model here is Odysseus' remark to the old maid after she sees the suitors have been killed in the *Odyssey*. What Chrysothemis refrains from doing is letting out a shout of celebration.

1246 *if it benefits...* Chrysothemis' use of 'benefit' (*opheleia*) marks this as an expediency position.

1266–67 *marriage / seems a fading dream at your age.* Elektra says that *Chrysothemis* will be unbedded (*alektra*)! See the note on lines 663–69.

1275 *profound and sacred respect...* Chrysothemis will get the reverence (*eusebeia*) of the dead. One of Elektra's key words.

1277 *noble.* The Greek word here is *eleuthera* (free). Chrysothemis claimed earlier (460) that she was free. Elektra has at this point stripped away all of Chrysothemis' rationalisations.

1303 *forethought* (*prometheia*) The chorus points out to the glaring deficiency of this speech. What Elektra proposes defies probability. Thus they prepare us for Chrysothemis' speech.

1304–5 *and if this were a rational woman / she would have stopped to think before she spoke.* Chrysothemis immediately uses two key words to a person of her character, 'rational' (literally 'wits' [*phrenon*]) and 'stopped to think' (literally 'caution,' [*eulabeia*]).

1334 *you cannot beat them: give up.* Elektra ended her speech with a heroic slogan: the noble prefer death to shameful life. Chrysothemis answers with one from the world of politics: the weaker must yield to the stronger.

1335 *Foresight!* (*pronoia*) The chorus has the values of any group and thus it places success above all. They cannot help but be alienated by Elektra's disregard of good sense. The result, dramatically, is to leave Elektra isolated at this point. She persists.

1342 *One hand will have to be enough.* A more literal translation is 'the deed is to be done' (*drasteon*). The use of the verbal adjective is typical of Sophoklean heroes.

1392–1466 The second stasimon consists of the chorus' praise of Elektra.

1436–8 *as a / killer / of furies...* The twin furies are Aegisthus and Clytemnestra, so called because of the ruin they have caused.

1437–41 *As a pure-blooded / child / of the father...* The word 'of good father' (*eupatris*) is closely related to 'born of good fathers' (*eupatrides*), a term used of the Athenian aristocracy. Elektra of course is literally 'of a good father' for by her behaviour she ratifies his virtue.

1467–1830 In the third *episode*, Orestes enters, Elektra laments over the urn, and Orestes reveals himself. Elektra and Orestes sing a duet. The Old Man enters, and the three characters speak, after which Orestes and the Old Man exit into the palace. Elektra gives a short prayer and follows.

1482 *Old Strophius sent me with news of Orestes.* Orestes seems to get the names wrong. Phanoteus is the one who is supposed to be sending the body to Argos. Although it is not mentioned in this play, elsewhere Strophius is said to be Orestes' ally and the father of Pylades. His error passes without being noticed. Perhaps it is a sign of his nervousness.

1614 *No! in all reverence...* Literally, 'not by your chin', a traditional gesture of appeal. It is a stage direction. Elektra holds the urn in one hand; she appeals to Orestes with the other.

1651 *You exist!* Elektra shifts into lyrics at this point, but Orestes speaks in iambic trimeter. Her joy knows no bounds, and Orestes keeps reminding her that there are bounds.

1846–59 This short song of the chorus is the third *stasimon*. They use traditional language to describe what has happened. The stage is momentarily empty – an unusual event in Greek tragedy.

1850 *the raw and deadly dogs…* These are the Furies. The language is traditional.

1856 *with freshcut blood in his hands.* An exact translation of this startling line.

1860–2008 In the final *episode*, or *exodos*, Elektra enters, and in a short *kommos* three excited actions occur: Elektra and the chorus respond to Clytemnestra's offstage cries; Elektra queries Orestes after he leaves the palace; the chorus see Aegisthus coming and Orestes re-enters the palace to await him. Aegisthus enters (the meter reverts to iambics) and speaks to Elektra. Elektra opens the door, and Orestes and Pylades exit from the palace with a covered corpse. Aegisthus, Orestes, and Elektra speak. Aegisthus enters the building, forced inside by Orestes. Choral comment.

Glossary

ACHAEANS   Homer refers to the Greeks as Achaeans or Dorians or Argives. Greeks refer to themselves as Hellenes. 'Greek' is the name used for them by the Romans.

ACHAEA   In historical times, Achaea was the name of a region located on the southern coast of the Bay of Corinth.

ACHERON   A river in the underworld.

AEGISTHUS   Aegisthus is the son of Thyestes. In revenge for a wrong, Atreus murdered the children of his brother Thyestes and, after feeding them to him, revealed what he had done. Aegisthus escaped the fate of his brothers and grew up to avenge this crime by killing the son of Atreus, Agamemnon. In Aeschylus' play *Agamemnon*, Aegisthus tells this story and claims that his cause is just.

AENIAN   The Aenians are a tribe mentioned in the *Iliad* as one of the contingents on the Greek (i.e. Achaean) side (2.749). Although they were involved in hostilities against the Spartans in 420 BC, they are probably here for the epic reminiscence.

AETOLIAN   Aetolia lies along the north shore of the Bay of Corinth, to the west of Delphi.

AGAMEMNON   Leader of the Achaean armies in the *Iliad*. In the *Odyssey* (Book 11, lines 404–34), set in Hades, he tells of his murder by his wife and Aegisthus on his return. Agamemnon and his brother Menelaus are the sons of Atreus.

AMPHIARAUS   One of the seven who fought and were defeated at Thebes, in support of Polynices' claim on the Theban throne. Polynices bribed Amphiaraus' wife Eriphyle to force her husband to go, and he went knowing that he would die at Thebes. In the battle, the earth opened and he vanished into the ground. He had more than one mantic shrine in Greece in historical times. The champion who avenged him was Alcmaeon, who killed his mother.

APOLLO   This Greek god has his main temple and oracle at Delphi, where games were held in his honour. The well-known statue usually called the 'Charioteer of Delphi', which was created about fifty years before this play was produced, gives us an idea of how the audience of this play would have pictured a driver in the chariot race at Delphi in which Orestes is said to have been killed. Apollo's oracle was often consulted by Greeks. His responses were often of a puzzling nature. Apollo's insistence that Orestes kill his father's murderers 'with a trick' is found in all versions of this story in tragedy.

APOLLO WOLFKILLER   'Lykaios', a regular epithet or cult name of Apollo, can be derived from *lykos*, the Greek word for wolf. The Old Man points out that the marketplace is named for Apollo wolfkiller (7–8), and Clytemnestra and Elektra both pray to Apollo as 'wolfkiller Apollo'. In Clytemnestra's speech (870) this phrase is simply translated 'Lycian Apollo'.

ARES   The god of war. His name often stands for violence of any sort.

ARGOS, ARGIVE   'Argive' is one of the names used for the Greeks by Homer. In this play, 'Argos' and 'Argive' refer to the region in which Mycenae is located.

ARTEMIS   Goddess associated with animals and the hunt, sister of Apollo. She is called 'unbroken' because of her virginity and independence. Women called on Artemis in childbirth. She hunted with her followers in the wild, and Agamemnon's boast was said by some Greek sources to have been that Artemis could not have made such a shot.

ATHENS   The only reference to Athens in this play comes in the report that the chariot from Athens won the race in which Orestes was said to have been killed. In Aeschylus, and in other versions, Orestes eventually stands trial for these murders in Athens.

ATREUS   The father of Agamemnon and Menelaus, who are called 'Atreidai' or 'sons of Atreus' in Homer and elsewhere.

- AULIS   Before sailing to Troy, the Greek fleet assembled at Aulis, a place on the east coast of mainland Greece and site of a temple of Artemis.
- BARCAEAN   Barca is a city in Cyrenaica in Libya. This is one of the two 'Libyan' teams.
- BOEOTIAN   Boeotia is a large plain north of Athens and east of Delphi.
- CHRYSOTHEMIS   Chrysothemis is said to be a daughter of Agamemnon, along with Laodike and Iphianassa, in the *Iliad*, 9.144–47.
- CLYTEMNESTRA   Clytemnestra, sister of Helen, is mentioned by Agamemnon in the *Iliad*, where he says that he cares for a concubine more than he does for her. Although his remarks occur in a bargaining context, they may hint at his later career. In the *Odyssey*, Agamemnon's ghost has much to say about her acts and how they reflect on women in general. She is the dominant character in Aeschylus' *Agamemnon* and plays a major role in Euripides' *Electra* and his *Iphigenia in Aulis*.
- CRISA   A town near Delphi. The hippodrome at Delphi is located below the sanctuary in more level ground. This region is known as the plain of Crisa.
- DELPHI   The mountain sanctuary of Apollo, where his main temple and oracle are located. Games were held here, which were one of the major athletic festivals in Greece. The oracle was consulted even in the fifth century. In the Greek historian Thucydides, a small Greek town asks the oracle how to end its civil war. Socrates says in the *Apology* that a friend of his went to Delphi and asked Apollo if Socrates was the wisest of men.
- ERINYS OR FURY   The Greek word for Fury is Erinys (the plural is Erinyes). These goddesses are depicted in Aeschylus, where they make up the chorus of the *Eumenides*, the third play of the *Oresteia*, as terrible-looking women with snakes in their hair. They prosecute Orestes before an Athenian court on the charge of matricide. In this play, there are several hints that Elektra and Orestes represent the Furies

of the traditional story in some sense. When Clytemnestra says that Elektra 'drinks her blood', that Elektra is something like a fury is clear enough. The chorus describe Orestes and Pylades as 'dogs' as they enter the house, and this is close to the concept of them in the *Oresteia*.

HADES   The lord of the land of the dead and husband of Persephone.

HERA   Wife of Zeus and queen of the Olympian gods. Hera in the *Iliad* is a strong supporter of the Argives, and her sanctuary not far from Mycenae was a major shrine in historical times.

HERMES   God who guides the souls of the dead to Hades, but in this story he guides the avengers of the dead. He is also a great trickster and a good friend of his half-brother Apollo.

IO   The daughter of the river Inachos and the ancestor of the royal line at Argos. Aeschylus tells her story in his plays, *Suppliants* and *Prometheus Bound*. Zeus conceived a desire for Io, and due to Hera's hatred she was turned into a cow, guarded by Argus, a creature with a hundred eyes. After Hermes had killed Argus, a gadfly drove Io around the eastern Mediterranean to Egypt, where she regained her human form and produced a child, Epaphus, whose descendents eventually returned to Argos and produced the line of Argive kings that included Perseus and Heracles.

IPHIANASSA   One of the daughters of Agamemnon in the *Iliad*.

ILYS   Itys is the child of Philomela. See the entry for Philomela.

LETO   The mother of Apollo and Artemis.

LIBYAN   Somewhat vaguely defined area on the north shore of Africa, whose main Greek settlement was Cyrenaica. This region does not figure in Homer.

LYCIAN KING   See Apollo wolfkiller.

MAGNESIA   A region in Thessaly. It is mentioned here because the Magnesians and the Aenians are both mentioned in Homer's great catalogue of forces in Book 2 of the *Iliad*.

MENELAUS   The brother of Agamemnon; the Trojan war was fought to regain his wife Helen after she had gone off with the Trojan prince, Paris.

MYCENAE   The traditional location of Agamemnon's palace, located on the northern edge of the plain known at the time of the play as Argos.

MYRTILUS   Charioteer murdered by Pelops, ancestor of Agamemnon. See Pelops.

NEMESIS   The goddess who repays excessive acts.

NIGHTINGALE   See Philomela.

NIOBE   Niobe (like Agamemnon in Elektra's version of the sacrifice of Iphigenia) let fall an idle boast and Apollo and Artemis killed all of her children, and then was turned into a rock formation.

OLYMPUS   A mountain in northeastern Greece, the home of the gods.

ORESTES   The son of Agamemnon and Clytemnestra. In Aeschylus' *Oresteia*, he went to Athens and stood trial for murdering his mother, where he was acquitted. In Euripides' *Iphigenia in Tauris* we are told that these wanderings continued after the trial.

PELOPS   The son of Tantalus, came to the south of Greece (later to be called the Peloponnesos or island of Pelops) where he obtained his bride by winning a chariot race by bribing Myrtilus, the charioteer of her father. As payment for his service, Pelops murdered Myrtilus and threw him in the sea. Pelops was the father or grandfather of Atreus and Thyestes.

PERSEPHONE   Queen of the dead.

PHANOTEUS   The ally of Clytemnestra and Aegisthus in Phocis.

PHILOMELA   Tereus married Philomela, and later raped her sister Procne. After murdering her child Itys to avenge her sister's rape, Philomela was turned into a nightingale, and she cries the name of her child 'Itys' obsessively. Sophokles wrote a play (*Tereus*) about this murder and frequently refers to the nightingale in his plays. In some versions the names of the two sisters are reversed.

PHOCIS   The region in which Delphi is located.

PYLADES   The son of Strophius of Phocis and Orestes' partner in his adventures. In Aeschylus' *Oresteia* he makes a single short speech. He is a major character, however, in *Iphigenia in Tauris* and *Orestes* by Euripides.

PITHO   Another name for Delphi.

SPARTAN   Sparta is a city located in the Peloponnesos. In Homer it was the home of Menelaus, by reason of his marriage to Helen, whose father had been king there.

STROPHIUS   The ally of Orestes and Elektra, and father of Pylades. He lives in Crisa.

THEMIS   A Titaness, who is associated with, and even stands for, law. Her name makes up the second half of the name of Chrysothemis.

THESSALIAN   Thessaly is a plain in north-eastern Greece.

ZEUS   The king of the gods. The nightingale is called 'the angel (i.e. messenger) of Zeus' in line 201. One explanation is that Zeus is the god in charge of the seasons (Horai) who are his daughters, and the nightingale announces the arrival of spring. However, the nightingale may be the 'messenger of Zeus' for another reason. The nightingale mourns the death of a relative, as Elektra does (1422–29), and so displays 'the reverence / of Zeus (1465–66)'.

www.nickhernbooks.co.uk

@nickhernbooks